TALKING WITH YOUR PEOPLE

A ROADMAP TO ACHIEVE BETTER
EMPLOYEE COMMUNICATIONS IN THE
CORPORATE WORLD

Ron Murray

MUREX PRESS
AUCKLAND, NEW ZEALAND

Ron Murray / Murex Press
1/34 Findlay Street
Ellerslie
Auckland 1051, New Zealand
Email: ducajiro34@gmail.com

ISBN 978-0-473-42981-2

Talking With Your People: A Roadmap to Achieve Better Employee Communications in the Corporate World examines:
- what is required for effective organizational/employee communications
- what is often missing or done badly in internal communications
- tools and processes – and practical ways – to improve internal communications within an organisation.

Key words: internal communications; organisational communications; employee communications; communications within businesses; change communications; human resources communications; health and safety communications.

Ordering Information: Special discounts are available on quantity purchases by corporations, associations, and others. For details, contact the author at the address above.

Cover concept: Cam Murray

CONTENTS

*Dedicated to every employee who ever felt left in the dark. There **is** a better way.*

Cinderella

Internal communications is the Cinderella of the communications world. Barefoot and rag-thin most of the time. External communications – principally corporate and marketing communications – generally gets the money and the glory. The drivers of the company's brand and image and the need to make money from products or services lead the agenda, win the big budgets and get to spend time with the agencies creating the campaigns that will hopefully bring revenue and a good reputation.

All of which is good.

But one of the biggest weapons in promoting an organisation's goals is its workforce (beyond the top tier of managers), and too often in business (or indeed in any organisation be it public sector, private or not-for-profit), communications inside the organisation, top-down, bottom-up, side-to-side, across the working units, is poor.

The inside stories don't get told - or get told badly or in an inconsistent way.

The internal comms* programmes, tools and policies may be in place – Cinderella has some clothes, a bed and they feed her – but they're often dysfunctional, under-resourced and neglected.

In under-emphasising or overlooking internal comms, organisations miss a big trick – employees feel no one talks to them, or worse - no one listens to them.   Their efforts in support of the company suffer from that dissatisfaction. It's a blow to productivity and engagement.

And we miss the chance to deploy an army of ambassadors for the cause: walking, talking billboards, fired up by the organisation's business and mission - and selling it to those they meet.

Get internal comms right though, and the reverse can occur. Put simply – happy staff, happy customer.

This guide to internal comms is about creating an environment that nurtures those billboards through fostering contented staff, who feel management keeps them informed and gives them real opportunities to make the internal conversation about the organisation a two-way (or multi-way) one.

Let's start the journey, pausing first to introduce your guide.

*I've taken the liberty of abbreviating communications to **comms** through this book largely because…it's easier to type (hah!) – but it's also readily recognised.

Ron Murray

I've been involved in communications since I was about two. We all have really. I'm one of the lucky ones who was able to turn an interest in readin' and writin' into something others value.

The career winds have blown me from an English major BA with a touch of Asian Studies through time teaching English and Indonesian at high school, journalism, public relations, marketing comms and comms management. Writing is at the core of what I do for a living, and it's also one of my main  recreational pursuits. You'd think I'd tire of it but, truth is, when you love to write, you never get weary of the trade. There's a pride in crafting each piece to a smooth finish.

My comms career has touched all bases, but the world of internal comms is a favourite space. It's the underdog; the waif. It cries out for attention and a better deal. Being part of an organisation and taking the internal comms to a higher level is immensely satisfying; all else flows from that.

My working world has been a journey across many organisations operating in a range of different sectors: engineering and energy, transport and finance, healthcare and forestry, banking, computers, the environment, not-for-profit. And every single space called for some internal comms TLC.

I'm a believer in the power of continuous improvement - and the truism that nothing exists that can't be made better. That's as true of internal (and external) comms as anything. I've titled this book *Talking **With** Your People*...not *to* your people only, you may have noted. It's a distillation of what I've learnt from almost three decades figuring out how to make internal comms (among other comms practices) better, for a wide range of organisations. I hope you find the journey interesting - and useful.

CHAPTER 1

Why bother?

In the Preface I touched upon the main rationale for having
a robust system of internal comms, summed up by the
phrase "happy staff, happy customer".

But how does good comms make employees happy?

1.1 THE GOOD

Let's go back a bit and think about what an organisation is.
It's a grouping of staff, ranging from a handful to perhaps
several thousand. It has a reason for being: providing a service
or products. It has customers it supposedly looks after and/or
stakeholders that it affects.

And it has a culture. A set of values maybe, best summed
up as "the way we do things around here." A style.

It has a reputation. Standing in the eyes of its stakeholders.
A good place to work (or not, perhaps).

Its employees are there 40 hours a week or more. They
live there for a great deal of their lives. They may have been
there most of their working lives. It is (or has the potential to

be) a second home, with a second "family". Workmates may become lifelong playmates (in all senses of the word).

Employees usually have good intentions of giving their all for the organisation. What they ask in return is that the organisation respects their working needs. And one of the biggest is a need to simply know what's going on in the business.

There's a simple security driver behind that: everyone likes to know their job is secure – or get early warning that it may not be.

But they also like to be kept informed about what's going on for four other very good reasons:

- it gives them a sense of "belonging"
- it helps them do their job
- it builds pride in the organisation
- it opens up the opportunity for them to contribute to the betterment and prosperity of the organisation and thus help shore up their job.

1.2 THE BAD

What usually happens in internal comms is often far from the ideal.

Sure, you may see the appurtenances of an internal comms programme; there's a newsletter (or many of them), there's an internal website (intranet), emails go out to staff, there are meetings, social events. Hey, we're communicating…What's the problem?

Problem is, simply having the tools doesn't guarantee communications is taking place. Common failings are:

- The intranet is like a fancy store, built with a flourish and initially displaying lots of content, but after a time the shelves can become bare of new goods and there may not seem to be anyone minding the shop.
- The newsletters look good but the news is flabbily written and old, the photos are poor, the real stories - the ones the staff would really like to read - don't appear, and the timing of the newsletters is irregular.
- The emails are poorly written, untimely, and not well targeted. Important emails don't happen or happen past the point of best effect.
- Meetings are poorly run, rife with bad behaviours, dominated by the loudest voices and resolving little. The all-organisation meetings - company updates and the like - are staged and stagey, one-directional by-and-large with well-scripted words coming down from on high and only a few brave (or eccentric) voices asking the curly questions.
- Organisations spread over a lot of locations struggle to get the messages around; foiled by the simple absence of a computer connection. Chinese whispers-style, the message morphs its way down through the management layers or fails to get past the middle management layer to the front-liners. The reverse occurs too − the troops ask for messages to be communicated up, but they die around half-way.

Such shortcomings in an external comms world would probably seriously hamper an organisation, but mediocrity seems to be tolerated in an internal comms world. After all, customers can choose to go elsewhere but employees don't always have that luxury. So they endure poor comms and just keep trying to do their jobs.

The blame for this generally must sheet home to management, though it's fair to say some employees steadfastly resist being communicated to, for various reasons. Common corporate attitudes around communicating with employees include:

- only communicating on a "need-to-know" basis
- not communicating *anything* because you can't communicate *everything*.

This tends to worsen at times of change such as a restructure. Precisely when employees want to know more about what's going on, they tend to get less information or shards of what's happening, and their senior managers tend to become somewhat invisible. There's a truism about bad news: people may not like it but they can come to *accept* it - particularly if it's an inevitable or unavoidable development and the rationale for what's happening is explained to them. They're much less forgiving about bad news *delivered badly*.

1.3 THE UGLY

There's an insidious comms black market that starts to operate when an organisation (in good times or bad) lacks good internal comms processes and tools: the rumour mill, aka the grapevine, or the water cooler club.

In the absence of sound information delivered by the leaders, the gap is often filled by conjecture fanned by the company gossips who thrive on the attention they get, or by the eternally negative souls in the organisation who, like

Private Frazer in *Dad's Army*, imagine - and pitch - the worst scenarios. There is an irony here though, because a significant, protracted silence at a time of change or crisis often *does* indicate bad news is in the wind; and that management hasn't the courage to prepare and front the story – or is getting advice to lay low and say nothing.

But the rumour mill usually is wildly out – promoting the worst-case scenarios. Only problem: in the absence of the truth (or information to the contrary), employees have no way of making that judgement call.

A sort of panic can set in: the comms become last minute, incomplete, error-strewn and imperfectly distributed.

Resentment grows. Resistance (to change) grows. Productivity takes a hit. Projects falter.

There has to be a better way. *There is.*

CHAPTER 2

Looking in the mirror

R ight. So you're the new Internal Comms Manager (or Adviser, if it's a small comms team). Or maybe you're the Comms Manager with no specialists to delegate anything to. Or worse still (gulp) maybe you're the HR Manager and comms has been added to your responsibilities (along with Health & Safety perhaps – I've seen that happen). Whatever your position, you've been tasked with sorting it out. Moving the organisation to a better space in terms of internal comms. Not always the glam job. Or maybe you're already there and you don't seem to be making much headway.

Hopefully the rest of this book will help you get to that better place – one way or another. But if you really want to make improvements to the internal comms in an organisation you must take stock of what's really going on. What's working and what isn't; what employees want. Too often communicators pluck the tool of the moment from the air and foist it on the unsuspecting audiences. A video, a brochure, a "Town Hall" meeting. For inexplicable reasons they rarely actually ask the punters how they would like to receive their information – or indeed what information they really care about.

That calls for an audit. But don't fill your mind with alarming visions of serious "suits" solemnly descending on the business, quizzing and grilling, disrupting and upsetting.

2.1 THE INTERNAL COMMS AUDIT

An internal comms audit is simply a questionnaire, sent via the likes of Survey Monkey, asking employees a series of questions about:

- what sort of information is *important* to them
- whether they are getting *enough* of it (or too little or too much)
- whether the *quality* of the information is good or not.

The audit also asks them to rate the communications channels that are available, seeks comments on the workings or effectiveness of those channels, and asks for suggested improvements.

When you boil down the results, the picture is very revealing: you soon see what's really important to staff in terms of information and what's *not* working in terms of how it's being conveyed to them (or what *is* - it's not always a negative picture).

A sample audit is attached in Appendix 1 (page 127).

I have a favourite story about the effectiveness of internal comms tools. The source was TJ and Sandar Larkin's excellent book on change communications *Communicating Change: Winning Employee Support for New Business Goals* (McGraw-Hill, 1994) - which is one of my recommended texts. The Larkins cited an organisation[1] - a US bank with around 40,000 employees - where the marketing team were weighing up the welter of comms channels and tools they had and wondering how valuable and effective they were. They included a monthly video, four newsletters, a personnel report (vacancies, promotions and transfers) and a social committee publication. Not a cheap raft of stuff to be putting together on a regular basis. Was it worth the spend? A bold person in the team suggested quietly stopping these tools - just discontinuing them without notifying anyone - and seeing what response they got. Which they did.

For most of the tools, there was a nil or single figure response after eight weeks; a handful of people at most asking what had happened to the video or the newsletter. The exceptions were the personnel report where more than 200 people asked what had happened to it, and the social committee publication which drew nearly 900 inquiries. Think about that for a moment.

We can get awfully bullish and smug about our beautiful websites too. A little auditing can actually reveal that some of those information-packed pages you slavishly developed haven't had a single visitor in years - if at all.

The lesson in both cases and it's another truism of the comms game: don't assume "message sent = message received". But more importantly, don't assume the information you think they want is the information they really do want. Ask them about it.

2.2 A REALITY CHECK

Executing an audit isn't necessarily a cakewalk (or a panacea); here are a few final thoughts on the process to bear in mind:

- Not everyone likes filling out questionnaires, so don't expect 100% returns on surveys; getting a statistically significant return may depend on the mood at your organisation and how well you persuade people of (a) the need to know how to improve internal comms, and - more importantly perhaps - (b) your commitment (or senior management's) to doing something about what they tell you. If they've pointed out numerous times in the past how you could improve and nothing's happened, you can expect an increasingly apathetic response to a survey like this.

- Most people are less than meticulous in their responses; don't expect beautifully crafted comments. But you will get a few very thoughtful and useful contributions. Consider hosting some focus groups post-audit, at which you can tease out more understanding of major issues emerging from it. Focus groups offer the ability to recruit participants from all the different parts of the organisation to get the range of perspectives you need.

- Expect more than a bit of mud-slinging, cynicism, anger, exasperation, vitriol and raw language; you're providing an anonymous outlet for it. Be aware that such voices may be speaking for a wider group. On the other hand, be aware that some people simply like to say things to please you and put an overly positive spin on their comments; tell you what they think you want to hear. Sheesh.

- In getting the audit out to staff, particularly where you have a mix of locations, roles, blue- and white-collar workers, high-technology access versus poor access and other obstacles – carefully work out your distribution plan, and don't forget to promote it, selling the "why". Emailing the audit link is straightforward, where people have email addresses (many often don't); those with addresses may also rarely look at their inbox – or just delete everything when they do, reasoning "if it's important they'll ring me – or come and see me." Getting paper surveys to employees is another option; if they have time to fill them out. See the challenges?

But definitely do an audit. Then analyse it and act on what it tells you.

CHAPTER 3

The challenges we face

If you always do what you've always done,
you'll always get what you've always got.
Henry Ford

E veryone knows how challenging it is to make your voice heard in the marketplace. Your customers are deluged by communications - ads, PR, salespeople calling, and all the new noise of the social media world like Twitter, Instagram, WhatsApp, YouTube and Facebook.

A different set of challenges faces the internal communicator.

3.1 THEM

Assuming you've successfully worked out what needs to be communicated and who you're communicating to (and with), making it happen can face a raft of obstacles:

- getting the information out of people who aren't convinced it's necessary or important or a good use of their time to give it to you
- getting the information around a diverse organisation that may be geographically separated, ie one that has branches, offices, depots or other functions in many different locations
- coping with the parochialism that the separation might bring with it.

The challenges arise from the sheer diversity of your workforce, ie:
- communicating the same information to office workers and field workers, white-collar and blue-collar employees, people on individual contracts and salaries and waged workers on a collective agreement affiliated to a union
- communicating the same information to shift workers versus those on regular hours, contracted employees versus permanent staff
- communicating with sub-contractors
- communicating with staff whose ethnic and cultural backgrounds may be very different, with attendant language issues and different cultural mores and values.

3.2 Us

But a good deal of the time, the biggest challenge for the internal communicator is simply to be taken seriously.

The standing of the comms department is often less than prominent. They don't usually have a seat at the top table - a common complaint - so can tend to hear late in the piece if anything needs sorting in a comms sense. It's a vicious cycle - you don't get told of issues in time, so the response may be less than effective, and the reputation of comms takes another hit.

That applies equally for external and internal comms; but internal is even further behind the eight-ball.

Few heads of departments, eg Human Resources HR), IT, Health & Safety (H&S), and Finance, enlist the help of comms to achieve their internal objectives at the outset of their planning. The internal comms team/person is often approached at the 11th hour to sort things out. They assume the role of "order-takers", and the comms actions probably come ready-formed for the team to enact - make us a brochure, a video, send out an email.

What should happen? Those responsible for the shared services functions within an organisation - the workings of which impact all employees - need to get internal comms alongside and planning jointly at an early stage.

The place to start is with what each department proposes to do in the year ahead (and this exercise should happen *before* the start of the new financial year). Call it their operational plan, their project list, whatever; but somewhere there should be a list of what the department intends doing to, for, or with, staff. Get that list and we're in business.

Each activity proposed - regularly occurring activities, new initiatives, unexpected (but often predictable) developments and issues - should prompt an assessment of the comms needs and objectives, and from there, a set of actions. You, the communicator, make that assessment. Order-maker, not order-taker.

This assumes there *is* a plan. If there isn't, or it's pretty fuzzy, things get a lot harder.

To make it easier – see Appendix 2 (page 133) for a simple communications plan template any department could use. It might just make the difference - for both parties. I'd also direct readers with a specific interest in one of those internal departmental areas to read *Chapter 6 – This section's for you,* where I delve more into the comms specific to HR, Finance, IT, H&S and other organisational functions.

3.3 CUTTING THROUGH

One of the biggest challenges in any subset of the comms game is getting cut-through – successfully getting your message to your desired audience amid the clutter of information bouncing around out there. It's like half-price day at the big clothing store – all elbows and confusion.

Henry Ford's quote to open this chapter was referring to business. If business is flattening - or worse, diving - you need to review what you're doing and how you're doing it. It applies equally to communications. If you're not getting much take-up, if it's a struggle to get messages across - it may be time for a change-up (to slip in a softball metaphor). A time to try something new.

3.4 KEEPING IT FRESH

There's a tendency to think once you've got your armoury of comms tools, you're set. But the world does move on; what seemed tried-and-true may well have become tired and dubious. Even very good comms approaches can suffer from becoming stale. New distractions arise to swing your audiences away from what you're trying to tell them. In the last decade, the competition for attention has become intense; the wild frontier of Social Media has opened up for everyone with something to say or the urge to listen, riding on the back of the technology explosion made up of cellphones, tablets, i-pads, wafer-thin lightweight laptops, Go-Pro cameras and the like.

There isn't an infinite array (yet) of new tools and techniques you can draw on to freshen up your comms. But there are a few things you can try. I'll go into more detail on those a little later in this book.

And here's another thought: don't let fear of failure hold you back. You have no choice if your comms is not having an impact - you need to do something; you need to try something new or different. Be bold enough to accept that a new way of communicating may not work perfectly or even well first time. But if you review how it went you may be able to figure out why it didn't have the effect expected - and revise the approach...then try again. Or try something different.

In Practice # 1 - Go west...

It's a major hospital rebuild in South Auckland. A lot of disruption and, in particular, parking is compromised on the site. But many employees don't realise there are plenty of carparks across the road on a separate part of the hospital campus – the Western Campus.

Western. Cowboys. Cattle-herding. You create a poster campaign around a cowboy/western theme. You and a willing accomplice don stetsons, vests, colts and mascara moustaches to distribute leaflets on the copious parking available over the road. The message is simple: "look to the West for a park." But the cut-through comes from the quirky posters (sample below) – known in common parlance as memes.

It works. People get the message and respond, taking pressure off the main site.

Cut-through. Crucial.

CHAPTER 4

Taking action

*Failing to plan is planning to fail. – **Benjamin Franklin***

*If you don't know where you're going, any road will get you there. – **Lewis Carroll***

*Content is king. – **Bill Gates***

Okay. The time has come. There's a need – maybe an urgent one – to communicate with some key stakeholders. You know what you want to say. There's a degree of agreement from those who matter that it needs to be said. Audiences are hanging out for their messages and dying to meet your objectives. (Yeah, right. You wish.)

But what *do* you do next? It's tempting to just roll up the sleeves and start banging out the information and sending it round the traps. But whoa up; there's an important procedural starting point.

4.1 A PLAN, STAN

Comms plans are often maligned. They get written but never get looked at. Management overrides them. What's the issue?

Not everyone is convinced of the need for a plan. Particularly if they're used to flying by the seat of their pants themselves. "Just make it happen" they say.

And in the absence of plans, things do happen – some good, some not. Things meander along in a haphazard way. Burning platforms take precedence. Comms' reputation takes another hit.

You can tell I'm in favour of plans, eh?

My comms colleagues will attest to that. I cite the Lewis Carroll quote at the start of the chapter. Not having a plan is fine if you're on an aimless journey, just going where the wind blows you. But comms management isn't like that. Or it shouldn't be.

A plan – however simple or complicated it is – is your roadmap. And a plan doesn't have to be complicated and technical. The simpler the better, in fact; you want your managers to understand it and help you implement it.

I use a seven-heading plan (attached in Appendix 2 page 133):

- Situation/Background
- **Objectives**
- Key Audiences & Key Messages
- **Strategies**
- Tactics, Tools and Channels
- Action Plans
- Evaluation

I've bolded **Objectives** and **Strategy** for a couple of reasons. First, they're the two most important bits to get right. Second, they're the two that most get confused with each other (and Strategies with Tactics).

Let's make one thing clear too: when I say objectives, for a comms plan I'm talking about communications objectives. Not business objectives or marketing objectives. Comms objectives are about moving your audiences down a continuum from knowing almost nothing about the subject to knowing just about everything and being right behind it, and there are a number of stops along that track – not everyone gets to (or needs to get to) the end point.

In comms talk, this is a journey along a continuum from awareness through understanding to acceptance, support and enthusiasm.

And it *is* a journey. Your job as a communicator is to work out where you need to take your various different audiences along that continuum. That becomes your objectives: at the end of your comms programme you should be able to measure in some way if you've achieved the desired level of awareness/understanding, support, or whatever your comms goal was – the Evaluation step at the end of my list.

You do that in a number of ways: surveys, polls, discussions, actions arising.

Strategy is your game plan or your battle plan for getting to those objectives with your set of key audiences. Strategies are necessary when your content is controversial or your audiences are many and varied and difficult to reach. If your comms is straightforward you may not need a strategy – it's just a simple equation around getting the messages in front of the audience.

But if it's more challenging you need to have a smarter approach. And your strategy will likely change depending on where your audiences lie on the awareness-to-enthusiasm continuum.

You can be more direct and factual when you're raising awareness but further down the continuum there will be an increasing need for active, two-way, face-to-face discussion.

There aren't a huge number of communications strategies it seems to me. Some of the more common ones:

- **Roadshows**. Taking the messages to the people on their patch. Leaders fronting and fielding questions. Powerful.
- Use of "**champions**". Empowering influential people within the organisation to carry the messages and model the behaviours – particularly if it's about change.
- **Special events**. Nothing so emphasises the importance of something as a special occasion where it's the core focus.

4.2 CUT-THROUGH

In the earlier chapter on challenges you'll recall my reference to cut-through. It's the essential goal of your comms: to reach your audiences effectively, to elbow your way to the front of the pack. To be compelling and interesting and relevant enough to be seen and heard - and remembered.

So how do you get cut-through?

No rocket science here: it's about content and about delivery. Probably in equal measure. Great content won't get cut-through from poor delivery; equally, poor content will not grab the listener no matter how groovy the delivery – except for those wowed by the smoke and glitter.

Have something important and relevant to say and then say it well.

There's a dilemma in comms (including internal comms): we often have set, regular comms vehicles, a newsletter for example, that we have to fill with interesting stuff. But interesting stuff doesn't necessarily arise in a set, regular way. The quality and strength can be up and down. You can have lean months - not much compelling to write up - or bumper times where it's "going off"- lots of great stories happening at once. What it means is that, at times, you can package and send pretty mediocre stuff. Which waters down the impact of the tool and the channel. We'll deal with this in a bit more detail in the section on channels.

But back to cut-through: having a great story to tell gets you halfway there. You must now deliver it in a memorable way. How do you do that?

You start with the writing - it has to be as good as you can get it. That means concise, clear, and vivid. Work George Orwell's Six Rules[2] - active not passive, short words not long, short sentences, etc. If your delivery is oral, there's even more need to be quickly comprehensible - the words don't hang around long.

Get visual. The world now thrives on moving pictures - snappy little wake-me-up videos. Lots of talk or walls of words will put your audience to sleep – or they'll divert their attention to the other channels they have open (cellphone, i-Pad, TV, X-box...) Even still photos will struggle for cut-through, especially if they're poor photos - badly lit, badly cropped, or just plain boring. More on this later (channels).

Who does your delivery? Pick someone with charisma. Someone trusted, respected. Someone who gets what you're trying to achieve. If they're delivering your messages face-to-face, cut-through will depend on how well they can captivate the audience. The TED talk phenomenon illustrates this - great speakers and great content, with the right kind of visual, generally equals cut-through. But remember, TED-talkers usually practice their talks hundreds of times, to the point where the delivery appears natural but is actually precisely scripted. And they keep them to around 18 minutes max.

Cut-through may be about draping a giant watch down a skyscraper as Swatch did once. Or as simple as sending a postcard with a great pic and a personal message, a technique I've used (sparingly) over the years.

The time to identify a cut-through approach is when you work through your comms planning and reach that point where you've figured out your objectives, confirmed your audiences and pinned down your messages...and you assess how hard it's going to be to do the comms.

If it's simple, you can probably work your tried-and-true channels; but if you identify that you have a real challenge in getting the message from A to B (C, D and so on), and need to work out a strategy or two...cut-through comes into the conversation.

Here's another thought too. Attention spans have never been great in a corporate world and they're probably less so now, as there's more chatter, more pressure to achieve your goals, and more going on.

People switch off very quickly if what they're hearing or reading doesn't connect with them personally or have some professional urgency. So a couple of things to remember:
- target your comms to those you think will be interested and for whom it's important and relevant
- get them involved - and by that I mean don't pour words and pictures on their heads for hours without giving them

plenty of opportunities to challenge, clarify, question, and support from their own experience.

In the "Looking in the mirror" chapter, I talked about the often-neglected approach to finding out what people wanted to hear or know - asking them.

If you package up your comms based on what people want to hear, structure the delivery so it's an efficient and involving discussion, and just invite those who need to be there to attend…you may get somewhere.

4.3   STORY-TELLING, JOURNEYS AND PANTOMIME

Any skilled primary teacher (or dutiful parent with little kids) will tell you how powerful an attention-grabber story-telling is. And there's a growing acceptance among communicators that one key to catching and holding an audience is to couch your messages in story form. Start, middle and end is a structure everyone gets.

Another way to look at this is to see the task as taking your audience on a journey. This is particularly valid in an oral communications setting – meetings, presentations – where the audience doesn't have the luxury of words in front of them (unless you're torturing them with walls of PowerPoint type – and much of the time they're disjointed, microscopic, jargon-ridden, poorly laid-out and generally unreadable).

What happened, why it happened, what happened next, what's going to happen, what it means to the listeners…that's a logical flow that works.

Another slightly different technique for cut-through that I've found very effective (and fun - which is sometimes missing from our game) is what I call *pantomime*.

Pantomime

Pantomime is a much under-rated and relatively uncommon comms tool. To some extent there's a temptation to want it to stay that way. As noted earlier, comms is an intensely competitive game and any advantage you might have over the plethora of other messages and information bombing your audiences is going to help you get your message across.

There are plenty of tricks or cut-through techniques, some of which work, though others can actually obscure or distract from the message, or create a negative emotion.

Pantomime is one of the former. The name is borrowed from the vaudeville tradition of England, but we're talking about something more adaptive and flexible. The core of pantomime in the comms environment is dressing up, acting out, and turning information into a story. It might have music; it might require some creative writing.

The point is to take a piece of communications and try to pump some life into it. Give it something to make people take notice of it. If possible, have some *fun* with it. That's a rough recipe.

The ingredients are the aforementioned content which you are trying to liven up, the occasion to roll out the pantomime, the players and the props. Not everything lends itself to this treatment, but many things do - and they thrive on the creative oxygen.

Here's an example: KiwiRail and TrackSAFE NZ ran a Rail Safety Week in August 2015 - a public campaign to raise awareness of the risks around the rail corridor and level crossings in particular. A simple message: "Expect trains". A worthy message and cause. But not a riveting or new story. We turned it into a rap ("Expect a Train"), which we recorded, then videoed a bunch of us (badly) lip-synching it and having a bit of fun near a rail line with trains going past (with a secure fence between us and the trains I hasten to add). The text of "Expect a Train" is in Appendix 3 (page 135) as a guide to the style.

A rap is a straightforward medium: simple beat, basic line and rhyme structure, and it doesn't have to be sung, just spoken in a staunch, strident way with a bit of attitude. You dress up a bit "gangsta", pull a few moves, maybe make a bit of a dick of yourself…but it doesn't matter. The words need to be clear and meaningful - that's the punch; the rest is just a colourful vehicle for getting it across.

Or you can pick any well-known, reasonably simple song and write your own words. You need a writer for that, but in my experience most organisations have at least one reasonably creative wordsmith or amateur poet - the trick is to prospect for that person early and nurture them.

And you need players - people prepared to step on the small company stage and go into role. You'd be surprised just how many budding amateur-theatrics wannabes there are in an organisation. I've role-played Mexican bandits (below), "Biggles"-style pilots, rappers, and Macarena monsters, and every time   I've very quickly found accomplices. They just need a leader.

Then there are the props: hats, costumes, wigs, and other items to add authenticity to proceedings. It doesn't have to be perfect: sunglasses and a mascara pen go a long way, but you may have to hire the odd item (sombreros for example).

There will be resistance to doing this sort of thing from some (stodgy) quarters but you need to be bold. Pantomime works best on occasions where there is a lot of information being imparted and the punters are hanging out for something lighter, like lengthy company conferences or day-long workshops.

It's a fair bet that, six months on, the oddball skit will be the thing people remember (mostly fondly).

4.4 CHANNELS AND TOOLS

If it's time to take action with your comms, you pretty soon have to turn to your armoury – and that means the channels to reach your audience and the tools you can use.

Communication is about the flow of essential or desired information from senders to receivers down a range of channels, and other information back the other way if that's what's needed.

Most organisations have some sort of suite of internal comms channels. They may even look pretty smart and function quite well. In the modern era, it's likely you'll find:

- an **intranet** of some sort (if the organisation's size warrants it)
- an IT system that supports **email** conversations - MS Outlook is the common one
- one or more **newsletters**, weekly, monthly, quarterly perhaps; possibly still printed, more than likely electronic (and emailed and/or posted on the intranet)
- a range of **meetings**, including perhaps an all-company meeting, departmental and team meetings
- a system (perhaps) of **noticeboards**
- a **social club** perhaps - yes, it's a comms channel (and a very important one for reasons I'll outline below)
- some level of **social media** perhaps, eg a LinkedIn community or some discussion forums, blogs and possibly Twitter activity; maybe a closed Facebook page
- **visual formats** such as videos, webcasts, podcasts, PowerPoint (torture) presentations.

These are the formal, planned and structured channels - or at least theoretically they are. But simply having a working channel doesn't guarantee communication takes place. Send some content down it by all means; but how do you know it reaches the intended listeners? How do you know they understand it? How do you know what their response is? How do you know it will have (or has had) the desired result of the communications exercise?

Truth is you often don't. Or you assume you do. Or you gauge the outcome from some surrogates.

The gold standard in communications is still face-to-face. Talking to or with someone or a group of people. Even then, you may be assuming the message is getting through when in fact it isn't, for various reasons I'll cover later.

Or your aim is two-way comms and you get a lot of nodding heads and some comments and questions perhaps. Successful comms? Don't bet on it. The default option for many people when they have something they want to say, or clarify, is to bottle it up, for fear they'll seem stupid or a stirrer. Or they just don't like voicing their opinions in a public setting. Or the people who do love to talk monopolise the time, and the session ends with a great deal unsaid and unasked. And silence gets taken for compliance.

There's another truism about comms that still holds: "Content is king" (as Gates said). Communicate when you have something important to say. You are competing for people's attention with an enormous welter of available information and distractions; weak, irrelevant, badly written, and/or dull content isn't going to get cut-through – and you know my thoughts on cut-through.

Channel choice is often ill-informed. A common error in comms everywhere is to choose the channel or the tool before really thinking through the message and the audience. How often do communicators get asked to "make a video"? Nothing wrong with making videos - in fact, they're kind of "the bar" in comms at the moment as people's preparedness to read text or even respond to a picture has waned - just look at what you have to do to catch attention on Facebook now. But is a video what you should be making?

The starting point (Comms 1.01) is your objective - what do you want to rev up the comms machine to do? Something must have happened or be about to happen that warrants the effort. Comms objectives are about moving people down the continuum from knowing zip to knowing lots, understanding it and responding in some way.

If it's a straightforward exercise, the conversation can turn to what you want to say (and to whom), and what channels or tools seem best for the purpose.

But if reaching your audiences is going to be challenging, you need to spend more time on the "how" and get more strategic, ie figure out what you can do to overcome the complexity of the comms challenge.

As noted earlier, objectives and strategy are two of the least well-understood terms in the comms lexicon. They get mixed up and often the subset of strategy - tactics - gets confused as well.

But it all stems from the objective. Remember Lewis Carroll: "If you don't know where you're going, any road will take you there." Making videos is fun. So is the arty thrill of creating a cool-looking newsletter.

But if the audience is 20 known people and you can get them in a room to hear (and talk) about the matter at hand, and give them plenty of time to respond - that's what you should do. The objective isn't to make a video or a flier.

Let's look at these channels in more detail.

The intranet

The intranet is one of the more complex channels and tools at your command. It promises so much but often falls well short of being effective.

The analogy I find most useful in trying to assess its functions and failings (and it applies to external websites as well) is the comparison with a new shop.

You set up a shop. New signage, new paint. Shelves full of stock, shop assistants bright-eyed and bushy-tailed (love that metaphor) behind the counter. Lots of marketing and opening-day specials.

Come back a few months later and unless it's taken off, chances are the shelves are barer, fewer people are on duty and the fizz has gone. Success isn't guaranteed from an early, one-off flourish of money, people and activity. You have to sustain it. If no one's in the shop and there's nothing fresh on the shelves, don't expect customers to flood in.

Intranets are the same. They are high-maintenance. Organisations must commit to having the resource in place to keep the shop open and the shelves stocked - with good, relevant content. That takes work and planning, commitment of resources in terms of people to do the writing – and passion from somewhere.

There has to be a game plan for the intranet. The technology enables you to create an endless world of clicks and links, but your customers aren't that patient any more. The intranet has to be a simple pathway for people to get the information they want or like - quickly.

Setting up an intranet calls for a clear plan: what do you want it to do? When your employees click to enter, what are they going there for? There tend to be two types of information on there for employees:

- information that's standard and, up to a point, timeless – policies, contacts, departmental resources, templates, etc
- information that's dynamic – news, event calendars, CEO blogs and so on.

In building your intranet, you establish places for both those types of information to be found via the front page. A lot of resource will go into locating and posting all the "timeless" stuff, and, over time, less effort is required to maintain that – just when things change. Conventionally, departments assign someone to keep track of that information and, in conjunction with the IT department, it gets updated in the normal course of things. You hope.

The dynamic side calls for a regular flow of content. Typically, you'll have places to post

- **news** about the organisation
- **events** – a calendar
- possibly some managerial **columns** like a CEO Update
- possibly an online **polling** device, to enable snap surveys of staff
- potentially some online **forums** (for want of a better word), ie places where employees can have multi-way conversations.

The presence of the last two functions will depend on whether there is a need. It may be that HR has alternative surveying functions such an Employee Engagement Survey via an external survey device, or employees carry out their organisation-related "chat-room" discussions via another medium such as LinkedIn or WhatsApp.

But don't necessarily expect to simply "build it – and they will come." In creating a website - internal or external - you are competing with thousands of other sites for employees' attention. It will get their attention if it delivers something they need or want by way of information – and can't get (or can't get easily) from anywhere else.

Comms teams have an advantage in having a lot of information about *what* the organisation is doing, *how* it's doing and *where* it's heading (most of the time anyway) and they are probably writing it up for both internal and external dissemination, so cutting and pasting it onto the website is relatively straightforward.

But don't forget: where online is concerned, short is good. Develop the ability to post summaries from which employees can "drill down" to get more detail, if they want the detail. More on this later (see newsletters).

Email

Email was quite a revolution when it first happened. Decades on it's still a powerful communications tool but as a fixture in your business life it's a mixed bag.

Imagine your letterbox with posties delivering 24/7. Piles of letters and parcels. How do you keep up? Email offers the same challenge; the wider your email address is known, the more email you'll get - and it'll trickle or deluge in round the clock. The inbox fills on a relentless basis and it's feasible in some cases that you could spend all your working day opening your emails and actioning them.

We all know of colleagues who solve this problem in the most efficient way: delete everything, on the understanding that "if it's important enough they'll phone me or come to see me." Or there are the legendary types who tell everyone they only look at emails once a week or some similar timing; same message. Phone me or see me.

Other people use Wan How's wonderful system of the Four D's: Delete, Delegate, Defer or Do[3] or something similar. That works if you're D for Disciplined.

In between, the great majority of us try to keep up with the inflow, constantly being distracted by the "ding" or the pop-up notification. Curiosity gets the better of us.

That's the view from the recipients' end. Half the problems arise from the other end - the sender. The mistakes here are:

- sending an email when a simple phone call would do
- cc'ing (or worse, sending directly) an email to someone who doesn't really need to get it
- sending an email with no call to action (what you want the receiver to do about it)
- sending an email that makes no sense
- not indicating in the subject line what it's really about (so the recipient can decide whether to open it or not)
- sending an email in a fit of anger or when you're tired
- sending an email that has an ambiguous tone
- sending an email when you should really just make a decision and act on it.

So helping solve the problems of endless emails is both about improving your own email behaviours and when others don't do the same, setting up some kind of screen or process to block the emails you don't want. The good news is that with the likes of MS Outlook, you can actually filter out all but the emails you really want or need, or at least manage the stream much more efficiently.

The Four Ds (above) is actually a very manageable solution, but needs to become a habit. A tour of what MS Outlook offers by way of canny tricks is also valuable. The path for the individual to gain greater control of their email isn't hard to find.

But for an organisation, the challenge is more profound. Sloppy email management affects morale and productivity in a number of ways: stress, wasted time sorting the mess, wasted time through poor communications being delivered via badly written emails, employees shutting down the channel because they're not on top of it. There are programmes to educate staff about good email management. Good luck with those. They're worthy but can feel a bit like a "re-education" camp.

There is a huge challenge too in organisations where significant numbers of staff don't have access to email. Any organisation with a mix of white- and blue-collar employees, with mobile, field-based staff often in remote areas with no internet access, can't rely on email to get the word to its staff. Often employees don't have an email address at all, or do in name only - no PC to pick it up on or wireless connectivity to do so. Or the speed of receiving and downloading information is slo-o-o-ow. In a world where we're all tuned now to ultrafast everythingband, waiting more than a few minutes - even seconds - for things to appear on screen often gets the thumbs down. Won't happen. We've become too impatient for the instantaneous.

But email is still a powerful channel, if used well.

"All-staff" emails do get messages out, but they better be compelling, relevant, well-written and preferably short.

Similarly emails from senior managers, particularly the person at the top.

Employees look for leadership. They expect it from those appointed to the highest positions in their organisation. And while they generally respect their leaders more for what they do – how they act – than what they say, what they say does carry a lot of weight. Leaders know more about what's happening, they know more (much more) about how the organisation is doing and where it's heading, and they usually know before everyone else if trouble is on the horizon.

Employees expect their leaders to keep them informed on all these things.

So leaders who never write all-staff emails, contribute think pieces to staff newsletters (or external publications), and rarely address staff or circulate talking with staff are missing the internal comms boat. Leaders are a channel for information – a very important one, perhaps the most important.

Worse still are leaders who are even less visible at times of change, for whatever reason. In a storm at sea, you expect to see the captain taking charge.

The smartest organisations hire leaders who are good communicators – internally as much as externally - and actively plan how that "channel" will be used.

Newsletters

Ah, the good old newsletter. Faithful, sturdy old flagbearer for the comms cause (internal or external).

There's an irony in the name of course: often what ends up in the newsletter isn't really news anymore because it's been around for weeks or months even…and most people probably heard about it through word-of-mouth. But at least there's a sense of the news being officially recorded, for posterity and all that.

Newsletters do make sense. Gather a bunch of information, write it up, grab some photos, pour it all into a layout, print it off and send it. It does fulfil a comms need in many circumstances.

And if the writing is good and the pix are clear and interesting, there's a good chance the readers will be happy. But that's a big "if". There are many ways a newsletter can fall short of ideal:

- It's too **infrequent** - quarterly or half-yearly for example – so, as mentioned above, it's probably not very newsy.

- It's **irregular** - despite best intentions perhaps, it comes out at unpredictable times, it's delayed, or issues are missed; the punters give up expecting it.

- It's too **wordy** - the stories are too long, too technical or too dull. Content is…you know the rest.

- It looks rushed and **unloved** – so why should anyone else love it?

- It's **anonymous** - there isn't the feeling that people produce it and it's about people; if there are photos of people they're miles away, unrecognisable and unnamed – or worse, wrongly named - anyway.

- The design is **unhelpful**: layouts are messy and difficult to follow, there are a host of different typefaces, colours and screens, the pages are too busy, and the writing is hard to follow in places because it's white type on a light screen…a cardinal design sin.

I paint a worst-case scenario, but many newsletters (or their editors and designers at least) seem to put obstacles in front of their readers wanting to get to the story.

I like the truism of design - "less is more" – a steal from the poet Robert Browning. A good newsletter designer knows how to make pages (and page spreads) work to ease the reader through the story comfortably. Keep it simple.

The electronic era has given us the perfect tools to make newsletters work for us. The favoured way to get one in the past was to receive a printed version. But over time, as more and more of the recipients gained access to the internet and familiarity with its delivery mechanisms, email arrived, then tools like Mail Chimp, and a significant flexibility came into the art of putting out a newsletter.

You could create a one-pager, with short summaries of your stories, and if readers want more they clicked on a link and drilled down to the detail - a paper on the topic perhaps, lodged on a website (or in "the Cloud"). That way you can take in all the stories without having to wade through endless detail you're not interested in and avoid lengthy scrolling online - still not the preferred way to read for many of us (…I'm showing my age here).

There's is a slight dilemma here, though, in terms of newsletter delivery. Electronic is fine - if you can receive it; the fall-back (if intended recipients can't access an electronic version) is to print it off and get copies around your unconnected sites. That's fiddly to do and not entirely workable if you've gone the drill-down newsletter route; it's much easier with the old-style full-stories newsletter.

Written or printed newsletters have a place but they're in competition these days with video newsletters - more on which later.

A final thought for this section anyway - you can waste a lot of money and time making fancy newsletters that hardly get read. These days you generally have to ask permission to send people electronic material - and make it easy to "unsubscribe". The same is not a bad tenet for newsletters sent to staff; the best approach if you set up a newsletter, particularly one with a specialised topic, is to get an example to people and let them choose if they want to keep receiving it. The "opt-in, opt-out" approach. As we used to say in magazine publishing – 'the best magazine is a wanted magazine'.

It's a double-win to do so: you reduce costs and you don't annoy people with unwanted inbox junk.

Meetings

Billions of words have probably been written or said about meetings. The fact remains that meetings are the heart of communications. The flagbearer for face-to-face information exchange. Real and immediate. In theory anyway. In truth, well-run and effective meetings are usually the exception. There's also a sneaking suspicion that meetings are often called when the convener can't make a decision. Then the meeting can't make a decision; it becomes a talkfest.

Sometimes the best decision made in relation to a meeting is *not to have one*.

Not that people plan meetings intending them to fail in their purpose. It's just that sometimes the purpose is a bit loose or vague.

Lack of a purpose is just one of a number of symptoms of a bad meeting. Others are:
•   lack of an agenda

- too short a notice to allow people to prepare (or poor preparation through busy-ness or laziness)
- late starts, poor in-meeting timekeeping and over-runs
- poor chairing
- people who roll in late
- people who bring their laptop or phone and work through the meeting, answering or sending emails or texts (mind you, if the meeting is a bad one – do you blame them?)
- people who say too much and crowd others out
- people who say nothing (when they have plenty on their minds)
- people who cut into or talk across others who are speaking
- discussion heading into irrelevant topics and not being reined in
- relevant discussion being allowed to drift into too much detail and not being taken offline
- no minutes (or poor minutes) being taken
- no actions being sought or arising.

These failings fall into two camps: bad organisation and bad behaviours; the first allows the second to happen.

It starts with the **convener** of the meeting who may be (but isn't necessarily) the Chair. The convener needs to have a good reason for dragging a group of other people away from what else they might be doing. The meeting needs to be a way of achieving some agreement, course of action or problem-solving that couldn't otherwise be sorted out without recourse to a meeting.

Let's say you've got a good **purpose**. And you identify the colleagues or other participants (such as a consultant perhaps) who will help transact the meeting's business. You invite them, give them the information they need to understand in preparation for the meeting, and allow them time to absorb it. And you locate a room and appoint a time.

So far so good. Next is the **agenda**. How's this meeting going to pan out? What do you (as convener) want to achieve from it - the outcome when the time is up? Blow-by-blow what do you want to happen during the meeting?

That's your roadmap. Now you need the driver: your **Chair**. Not everyone can be the Chair. It needs to be someone prepared to control the meeting in the best sense of the word. Someone who has the respect of the participants and the ability and willingness to keep them firmly and fairly in line; to allow the discussion to go where it needs to but steer it back quickly to the agenda when it meanders (as it will). A good Chair is the key to a meeting's success.

The Chair should curb the bad behaviours and set the tone for the meeting. That means starting it on time and ending it (unless there's a very compelling reason to extend it) on time, hopefully by carefully managing coverage of everything on the agenda to fit the timeframe; not allowing people to join the meeting when they choose, unless they only need to be there for a specific part of the meeting (which is entirely sensible); and acting on all the bad behaviours listed above.

Some of those are easy to remedy; others take a bit of work. One of the hardest to sort out is the silent person who actually has a lot stored up to say, feels strongly about it but for some reason says nothing. This may be because others are dominating proceedings; or the silent person simply isn't brave enough to speak out - or feels doing so is futile. The Chair (or another nominated participant) needs to probe for the unspoken thoughts and feelings at a meeting - the Yoda role as author/entrepreneur Keith Ferrazi described it in a *Harvard Business Review* article[4] - and call them out.

Meeting participants should understand the poor behaviours and why they're not to be tolerated; how they sabotage the meeting's purpose and chances of success.

The Chair needs people in the meeting who back the discipline. He/she also needs a **Timekeeper/secretary** to keep track of the discussion and, importantly, record the actions, timings and responsibilities.

That's a generic meeting. It could be a project meeting, a team meeting, a marketing meeting...any gathering of people to discuss and sort something. If you want a very basic mnemonic to remind you of what a good meeting needs, think **PACT** – Purpose, Agenda, Chair and Timekeeper...and make a pact with yourself to at least run *your* meetings with that core framework.

In the internal comms world, meetings serve the purpose of getting information across to those gathered, finding out information from those gathered, or more commonly: a mix of both.

They range from a simple team meeting where the manager imparts essential information to the team, gets their feedback, answers their questions and advances the company culture along the way, through larger gatherings - business units or support service divisions - to the full-blown all-company gig, sometimes called a Town Hall meeting.

The Internal Comms Manager isn't expected to run every meeting, nor would they want to, but since it's an important communications channel they should influence how well meetings are run.

Company updates

There *is* one sort of meeting, however, that is their domain (or should be) - the all-organisation meeting or **company update**. And that can be a challenge. Let's take a look at what's possible in that space.

First, the numbers within the organisation and where staff are located – how dispersed they are – will dictate to some extent what's possible. The spectrum includes:

- a relatively small number of staff in one location – say up to 100 across one or more floors in an office block, or across an industrial site
- two or more sites with large numbers of employees in the same city
- relatively large numbers of employees located at multiple sites in different cities; a bank network for example.

The spectrum becomes more varied when you add in a blue- and white-collar split, a field force who work out of home, or the organisation's sister sites in other countries – Australia, other parts of Asia, Europe, the Americas.

The audience you have to reach dictates how you will best do it; if your workforce is dispersed a roadshow may be required.

The tighter and more intimate the meeting – the less distance between the speakers and the audience and the more interaction – the better.

There is probably a tipping-point type number (150 people?) where the dynamic of a meeting changes; where, as a participant, you begin to feel like part of a crowd at a rally. Over that magic number, the meeting is essentially one-way communications; the follow-up – team or departmental meetings – becomes crucial to the comms succeeding. But below that number, the dynamic can be managed to make the meeting effective. In my experience, this recipe works well:

- Combine the meeting with refreshments – morning tea, coffee, water, juice, finger food. People gather, get something to eat and drink, chat briefly (a valuable, inter-disciplinary communications opportunity in itself) then move into the meeting room.
- An hour max.
- No more than five or 10 minutes on each item, with lots of different speakers.
- Probably no more frequently than every two months; monthly is do-able but they're a lot of work and that regularity may not be necessary – it may be a stretch to get enough content to warrant bringing everyone together.
- The CEO should be one of the speakers, and they (and their management team) should always try to be present. If they're not (and could have been) it suggests the meeting is unimportant; and the audience will treat it as such.
- Form the chairs in semi-circular rows – the centre of the semicircle being where the speaker will be positioned. Think "theatre in the round" – Bill the Shake, the Globe and all that. Stagger the chairs so that people are not staring into the nape of the person in front of them. Intimacy and closeness. Distance and separation has a metaphorical as well as physical dimension.
- Ban PowerPoint – or at least ban wordy, detailed slides no one can read or that the speaker reads (ghastly). Slides with striking visuals are okay.
- Start with the CEO's/GM's/MD's regular state of the nation – how we're doing, and what's ahead.

- Let staff know well in advance that the meeting is happening and call for suggested topics.
- Have a question and answer session early in the meeting – after the CEO's slot is good; he/she will have prompted some queries. The rationale for doing it early, rather than – as usually happens – the Q&A being the last item on the agenda, is that you usually run out of time at the end of the session, people are tired of the talk, and are keen to get back to work or have other meetings to go to. So the most important part of the whole gig is cut short or (worse) doesn't happen.

I'm going to dwell a bit more on that last point. Company gatherings may be seen as being good, democratic, two-way communications, but in reality they usually fall well short of any of those adjectives. Honesty and transparency are almost always on the shopping list of Values organisations hold dear, but the rhetoric is often more compelling than what actually happens. Company updates are straightforward if the news is good, and things are going swimmingly; but if there are issues afoot or there's bad news, there's a strong management inclination to tug the cards close the chest and clam up.

Q&A time can be when the hard questions, the curly ones, might come up. And there's a very interesting phenomenon that occurs in organisations in relation to this. Individuals come to the fore who can generally be expected to ask those questions at Q&A time to the point where the organisers semi-jokingly will ask if those individuals have a question they'd like to ask. I kid you not; I've seen it happen time and time again. Thank the stars for those people. They are courageous enough to ask the questions that everyone else may be wondering about but isn't game to ask – in case they look like a stirrer. Or a know-it-all.

Sadly, the company update is one of the very few occasions where you *can* put your senior management on the spot – gently or otherwise - over something that's important. But time and time again, such meetings finish with very little two-way discussion…and lots of unanswered questions.

Noticeboards

If internal comms is the Cinderella of the comms pantheon, the humble noticeboard is the Cinders of the internal comms family.

In any office, depot or other workplace gathering-space, there's likely to be at least one noticeboard. A space where all manner of pieces of paper get pinned and generally stay there till they wither on the pin and fade to illegibility, and are put out of their misery by some kindly soul.

Noticeboard comms is usually haphazard, unplanned and ungoverned.

Which is a huge shame because they do have a place in the internal comms armoury - quite an important, and in some ways unique, place.

Noticeboards may lack the 21st century vibe of the intranet or social media channels, or the power of a great company meeting or an attractive, newsy, company bulletin. After all, they're just a piece of vertical comms real estate. If nothing's up there or there's nothing relevant or interesting, it's like the Samsung 42-incher when it's turned off. Nothing happening.

But noticeboards are often in places where important comms can and does take place between employees: cafeterias, smoko' rooms, halls, lounges.

Often these are field or workshop employees - blue collar workers - who don't have ready access to the "suit suite" - laptops, smartphones, tablets, email (at least not at the organisation) - and are hard to reach as a result. But during the day they take breaks and head for the company tearoom. Where the noticeboards are.

If there's something on the noticeboard, especially if it's something new and doesn't look boring, it will generally catch their attention. If it's not camouflaged.

So grab the opportunity.

Noticeboards come into their own if you get two things right: the content and the management.

Scruffy, hard-to-read, nondescript notices will struggle to capture the punters' attention - and when they do turn their gaze to the piece of paper that's pinned there, like as not, it doesn't tell all the story or tells it poorly.

What goes up needs to be written well, concisely, in a readable-sized font, with something to catch the eye - an illustration of some kind to break up the blocks of type.

That's the theory anyway. Truth is, all sorts of documents will end up pinned there, the same way rubbish will keep piling up at the back of the shop if there's no system of removing it. That issue we'll cover below.

Ideally, what goes up should be readily readable from a short distance. The best candidate for that is a simple, well-made poster. The bigger the better - up to maybe A2. A3 and A4 will work OK. Bullet-points, big bold pictures. Contact information. A call to action.

There is no shortage of content suitable for a noticeboard; the issue is just getting it into a format that works on the wall.

If you really take your noticeboards seriously, you probably need to have a few around the premises. Typically you'll find a social club board and an H&S one, or there may just be a few, random, "throw everything at me" boards.

If you really want your noticeboards to work, they need to be managed. In simplest terms, someone has to be in charge of them. A gatekeeper of sorts, putting relevant material up and taking it down when it's no longer relevant.

Either you as the comms patrol do it, or you encourage the habit among the managers you work with.

If a noticeboard post is part of your comms plan for a particular project – its removal date should be in the plan.

Social clubs

What's a social club? In most, if not all, organisations there is generally a core of people who like to actively socialise as workmates or colleagues. It's only human nature. You work with people, share interests, make friends. You work hard, share the joys of business success, or endure the tough times together. Plenty happens in an organisation of a social nature.

Yet social clubs often struggle. They have a somewhat unprescribed place in an organisation. The company management often leaves it entirely up to staff to run the social club; a benign employer may support the club, by subsidising activities or other costs. The place and status of a social club is not often written into the company structure.

It's left to the usual tireless, personable crew of employees, who like organising events and having fun, to make things happen. And they do. Picnics, family days, quiz nights, outings, sports events, charity activities. Not everyone gets involved in everything, some don't get involved in much at all, and there will always be a percentage of staff who don't want a bar of it. They come to work to work - and socialise entirely away from work. Fair enough. That's their choice and their right.

But the fact remains that a good, thriving social club is an asset to an organisation. It brings fun, exercise, involvement, and friendship to the lives of people in the company, supplementing what their private lives provide in that respect as well, but often filling a gap in some people's lives.

They also provide an incredibly important comms channel within an organisation. Any internal comms practitioner should understand how social events can help get information around an organisation. It's not cool, of course, to try to pour corporate messages into social occasions, but they are times where what's happening in the company does get raised, discussed, and critiqued. Questions about organisational matters get asked, and out of the cluster of participants an answer may arise. Is it accurate? Not always, but the channel is there, with the opportunity to state the truth and scotch the rumour.

What makes social club events even more interesting to communicators is that they provide one of the few occasions when employees from different parts of a company mix - Finance with Sales, HR with IT and so on. The exception perhaps is the typical company end-of-year dinner where teams tend to want to congregate at tables with their close teammates (and partners). At other times they do mix and that "cross-pollination" (figuratively speaking!) opens the opportunity for people from different parts of an organisation to learn about what their distant colleagues do and think, and how they all contribute to the organisation's goals.

Where social clubs and social events are concerned, your strategy as an Internal Comms Manager is to become involved and encourage others to do so, particularly the organisation's senior management. If you do take part, and your managers do likewise, there is the potential for valuable, truthful conversations to take place, working relationships to develop and improve, and issues to be resolved, purely through the medium of conversation over a drink at a barbeque or on a charity walk.

If management get involved in the social activities, there's an acceptance that from time to time they might "say a few words" with the accent on "few". They mustn't hijack the occasion to bore or browbeat anybody. But the comms team should be alert to misinformation arising, or unnecessary concern surfacing about the organisation on these occasions – it's a valuable opportunity to gently put things right.

Social media

Talk communications of any flavour and it won't be long - maybe nanoseconds - before the topic of social media comes up. It's been around for a while as a descriptor but probably doesn't accurately capture the multiplicity of tools, channels, "apps" and other modern phenomena that seem to fall under the name.

It's termed social because it grew out of the proliferation of electronic comms tools - the cellphone in particular - that enabled people to quickly, simply and cheaply talk to each via voice or text, exchange photos and videos, and socialise.

The social media family is all pretty much common knowledge now: Facebook, YouTube, Twitter, LinkedIn, Instagram, Pinterest, SnapChat, Yammer, and so on. New ones emerge onto the scene all the time. Ways of connecting people, and that's the core of it: these were new ways for people to create a sense of community - their own big or small gathering of like-mindeds - and communicate. You "followed", you "liked", you re-Tweeted, you posted. You connected.

The action was principally around socialising, but the marketing world caught onto the opportunities offered by the social environment and started elbowing its way in. The rest is history. The socialising carries on, but there are ads, and that new blend of info that comes across as fact - but is, deep down, pure marketing, hoping to go viral.

So what's the application to a business environment? How do the social media tools fit into the day-to-day business of internal comms?

Gingerly, I'd have to say. That very question has left many internal comms practitioners scratching their heads, and their corporate masters (who sign off on the IT policies and the costs) being very dubious about encouraging too much indulgence in the distractions posed by Facebook browsing and "liking", Twitter "following" and YouTube surfing.

There are two questions: What can you use these tools for? And how can you implement them?

Social media tools are a platform for communications within a discrete community, so theoretically you could establish a private Facebook page for your organisation - or subsets of the groups of like-mindeds within it, such as your "greenies", or the social club (which logically should communicate via social media). The same applies for LinkedIn: increasingly the location for groups with a shared, more business-oriented interest. It's a well-established process: create the group, seek members, have an administrator and rules of behaviour, light the touch paper and stand back. If the group has something urgent or important to talk about it probably will. That's a big "if". If there isn't a compelling reason for the group members to want or need to communicate via the Facebook page or LinkedIn group, they won't, and it'll wither on the vine.

These are very liberated comms channels. You can get information and messages up online, but your audience is not a passive one; they will not react well to the channel being used for propaganda – and they can respond aggressively (though perhaps not as viciously as in the external social media world). They do provide a reasonably powerful medium for people to exchange views and information. They are catching on, but much more slowly in the internal comms environment than they did, and are, in the wider world. Up against the power of email and the simple art of a good meeting or newsletter, they haven't yet demanded a prominent or essential place in the internal comms pantheon but that may change over time. Many Comms Managers can't quite see how to blend them in and senior managers are not generally convinced.

If you do want to bring them into the fold, the best place to start is with some identification of the actual community they will serve. If you have a group with shared interests with comms to do, maybe a LinkedIn or a Yammer will work. Find a passionate individual or individuals to run it, and you may be in business.

But start with the need. Then if nothing else in the comms armoury can get the comms going you want, consider what the social media tools and channels can do.

Visual formats

We live in a communications world that is increasingly dominated by visual media.

Everyone with a relatively simple and inexpensive phone can take photos and play with them then send them virtually anywhere; the same phone can take videos and allow you to edit them and supply a soundtrack - and send them anywhere. And tens (maybe hundreds) of millions of people globally do exactly that. Facebook, Instagram, YouTube and their like are the movie theatres and photo galleries of the modern age. Selfies and short movies abound. Thirteen-year-olds have online video websites dispensing their own brand of wisdom - and advertisers pay them to run their ads on the site. Add in the Go-Pro and drone phenomenon and everyone can be a Steven Spielberg.

When you try to get your information and messages across internally (or externally) that's what you're competing with. A massive barrage of images and videos pouring down on your people - along with screeds of writing. The sheer volume of content available means you have to work very hard to break through and catch their attention. The phenomenon of "click bait" has emerged as media float tempting morsels of "news" trying to get you to enter their world (and view their ads). Your employees are both spoiled for choice and probably time-starved so they're very choosy about what they focus their attention on; and it better deliver, or they'll switch off and turn something else on. The qualifier to this is that the new generations are much more adept at multi-tasking where media are concerned than previous ones: watching a movie, listening to music, playing a game, texting...the brain is plastic enough to enable people to be attentive to multiple inputs. But they're less patient; if it's not captivating, and satisfying an immediate need or interest, they will look for something that will.

It's interesting to observe how Facebook has evolved in this regard. Written posts used to work fine, with the occasional image. Then everything needed an image to catch the attention. Now every second post at least has a video – and it starts automatically. The ante has been well and truly upped.

Photography

So visual media has a definite place in your armoury. Which means you either need to develop the internal skills and resources to photo and film, or have a readily available and reliable supplier to generate your visual content. The good news is that most organisations have plenty of amateur photographers and film-makers (and more than a few who could well do it for a living – and possibly do in their spare time). They often have superb gear and most of the time are happy to snap for you - as long as it doesn't jeopardise their probably already-very-busy day job.

Digital technology makes it simple to take as many photos (or films) as you like; your only limitation being how much memory your device has via its internal storage. The sky is now literally the limit as you can also feed your high-resolution visual files to the Cloud. So you can snap almost every moment of interest or importance to the organisation.

What do you do with it? Essentially, you're generating the key visual content for a host of common internal comms channels: your intranet (and external website), your newsletters, presentations, posters and so on.

Still pictures struggle to compete with the dynamism of video but there's still a place for memorable shots. An initiative that goes down well that you might to consider is the stills highlights reel run at the end-of-year party or final organisational meeting. This might be up to five minutes long, with backing music, and typically tracks the year in pictures – the vast majority of which should be people pictures. You can have some fun, tastefully and gently tease people about the highs and lows, note the good times and respectfully honour the dark moments. Light and dark. Honesty. Powerful, believe me.

There are two other visual format modes of communicating that have some potency in an organisational setting: organisational videos and framed photos.

Video

Organisational videos come in two shapes - video newsletters and instructional videos. The first are simply a version of the good old printed or electronic newsletter but with scripted, filmed content - stories. No rocket science in that. But they still require the editorial discipline of any newsletter. They take a lot more work and cost more but are very popular if done well.

How do you do them well? The same short film-making disciplines that apply elsewhere - keep it short and sweet and don't bore people. Identify your editorial plan for each video - the stories you'll cover and who will deliver them on camera - then start organising. You have to book people, arrange locations, brief your "talent" on what you want them to talk about and then do it. Weather and other unplanned disruptions will muck you around, but ultimately you'll get a load of raw footage. Which then has to be edited. That's where the crafting takes place; your editor needs to know what you want and also how to weave the stories into one fluid piece. An internal newsletter needs to be no more than about 10 minutes; preferably between five and eight. That's plenty; especially if you need to slot the showing of the video into a tight team meeting.

What should you cover? Your people - and if you do these regularly, one a month for example, make sure you range across the wide richness of your organisation's people and activities. Be democratic (in the sense of planning) and try to shine the light on everyone at some point in the cycle - geographically dispersed, white- and blue-collar, and across all business units and shared services departments.

And have an editorial plan: each video should hit some important cultural touchstone or some strategic imperative - diversity, H&S, leadership, whatever - you decide. But don't make it too "corporate", slick or preachy – get real people on camera telling their stories. It works.

Instructional videos are just that: you film something being done - to show others how to do it. This makes it much more real than a 60-page, A5 booklet. The same rules apply as for any comms though: tell the story - script it well, get good natural talent, and rehearse them but try to let them tell it as naturally as possible - otherwise it feels wooden and forced. Get people who believe in what you're filming and let the passion come out.

Framed photos? What's novel about that? But here's the thing: we generate so many opportunities for a great commemorative photo, yet it's rare that we actually make the most of it. That great sales deal being signed? That team-day moment? That notable milestone? Snap it and put it in a frame, with a caption/citation. Do 20 and give them to the team. Gold.

The picture on the wall does several things: it reminds people of their success and their great moments; it reminds others; it captures in time great teamwork and friendships. Otherwise this stuff is lost to the ether. Hidden away in increasingly jammed memory-banks. Bring it out, dust it off - celebrate it. Forever.

And plan this in advance. If it's a last-minute thing, you might miss the (organisational) moment.

4.5 BREAKING THE RULES

This has been a long chapter and if you've made it to here, well done. But I wanted to close this chapter with a quote from my boss at a health authority I worked for in the early 2000s.

Dave Clarke was a visionary CEO – he gave us all a copy of the Larkin & Larkin book on change communications I referred to earlier – and he knew the importance and power of cut-through and the need, at times, to leap right outside the square and do something different or differently. His words to me one day when we were contemplating a piece of challenging communications? *"You know the rules, Ron. Break them."*

Dave – if you read this, rest assured I did...from time to time. And survived.

In Practice #2 - The foyer pic

Siemens builds wind farms. In New Zealand that includes the first Siemens installation, West Wind, at Makara on Wellington's southwestern coast, and later its sister installation Mill Creek to the north. Visitors flying in and out of the capital see them clearly (if the weather is good).

A photographer (Rob Suisted) gets a superb panorama photo of the farms from the air – it appears on page 1 of the local daily. You order a 2m by 1m canvas of the photo and install it in the foyer.

Pride. We…did…that.

CHAPTER 5

Who does the work?

P lenty is possible in internal comms and it's eminently
justifiable, so let's rip into it. But wait…who does the
work? Here's where we strike a few more potholes in
the road.

5.1 THE TYPICAL SETUP

Your typical comms department is generally a pretty lean
affair. Depending on the size (population) of your
organisation and the extent to which the people at the top take
comms seriously, you might have anything from one to a
dozen or more comms staffers. Having no full-time comms
people in a relatively large organisation in New Zealand is not
uncommon. If there is a team, however, there'll likely be a
Manager (or Head of Comms), and maybe one or more
Advisers, Officers or Executives, possibly with some
specialty affixed to their title like Public Affairs, Media or
Government Relations, along with an Administrator/PA

perhaps. There may be some specialist operators like a designer or events organiser. Small teams tend to include people who do most things that fall into the comms brief.

It's rare in my experience to find someone with a purely internal comms role but they do exist, particularly in larger organisations with major challenges in getting the words to the people.

That person (or whoever gets nominated to include internal comms in their portfolio) needs to understand the channels operating, be good at developing and maintaining good relationships – you will be surrounded by "clients" – and be pretty sharp at stringing words together, quickly.

They need to have a friendly designer on the team (or on tap) and be on particularly good terms with the organisation's IT people.

They need to be committed to the cause of internal comms and progressively more and more embedded in what's happening in the business.

Internal comms isn't usually something agencies specialise in to a great extent, and there's a reason for that. Because it's a Cinderella function in many organisations, the fees on offer for internal comms work are similarly likely to be Cinders-like. Proving an ROI on the glamour comms tricks like media work and advertising, digital campaigns and marketing collateral support, is more straightforward. It's harder to show the dollars back to the company from keeping their people happy and well-informed.

So agencies can tend to be order-takers on internal comms stuff: keep the website loaded, put together our newsletters, help organise our roadshow. It's a brave agency that challenges the existing order of things, because these are tangible, billable, profitable pieces of work. An agency is unlikely to tell you to quit producing the newsletter because it's a wrong option for the comms you're trying to do – unless they are savvy, and brave. Adventurous internal comms stuff is difficult to sell at the best of times; tougher still for a consultant. That's not a universal claim I hasten to add – there are agencies and consultants with the skills, knowledge, panache and moxie to do great work in this area for their clients. But for the reasons above it's not that common and it's not uncommon to find patchy internal comms in an organisation that is otherwise well-served by an external PR agency. And more often than not that's because the client's management team doesn't rate internal comms as a priority, which makes it hard for the agency to.

5.2 EVERYONE IS A COMMS MANAGER

Everyone is a Comms Manager. A provocative statement, I hear you say. But to my mind it's true. We *all* manage communications all the time; we just don't all have the title within our organisation. We all speak and write and exchange information at home, work and play. Of course we manage communications.

But people persist in believing that, in an organisational environment, all comms is "done" by the comms department. That's like saying all budgeting should be done by the Finance team; or all health and safety by the H&S team. Rubbish.

All managers should aspire to the point where they manage their own communications at work, based on sound comms principles and plans, supported in a consultancy sense by the in-house comms experts or their external advisers.

Commonly the biggest call will be on strategy – deriving the game plan to make a particularly challenging piece of communications happen, writing ("wordsmithing" as it's commonly called) and designing, media management, issues management, and possibly event organisation – though skilled PAs and administrators can organise events. In an ideal world, managers would innately understand what they need to do to carry out a piece of comms and plan and implement it accordingly. In an ideal world.

Till then, an achievable goal is simply to convince managers of the need to plan their communications with the comms team's help, and make some effort to improve their own personal comms skills. I'd possibly settle for that; it also means Comms Managers keep their jobs. Don't want to tempt Finance too much.

But that *does* mean actively developing their skills. To be a manager you would expect they will have received training in the skills required to manage and lead. And they generally do have training in how to plan and implement, lead and motivate, budget and account, and reward and discipline. But in my experience they don't get a lot of formal comms training, certainly not once they're in the role. They do have plenty of innate skills, derived from their working experience, and with varying shades of capability they run meetings, send emails, give presentations, prepare reports and possibly talk to the media. All tactical stuff. What's missing is a sense of comms planning.

Which we comms types should be able to give them. Appendix 2 (page 133) has an example of a simple template that, if you follow it, will bring at least a rudimentary element of planning to *any* comms you want to do as a manager (or as an anyone, really...Everyone is a Comms Manager remember?) The template applies as much to internal comms as external comms.

There can be a particular shortage of comms skills in managers at times of change. But managers have a huge role in making change succeed, through their modelling of behaviours, their support and understanding of the rationale for change and their support for the heightened need to demonstrate "care" for the employees through tough times.

The Internal Comms Manager should actively seek to proselytise his or her skills and techniques. In the absence of a comms (let alone an internal comms) team, the managers of the organisation *are* your team. So you help them be great at it.

Unions

Organisations with a union presence generally have another very important communications asset. That's the union's own communications systems that operate alongside the organisation's systems, and if internal comms isn't working with them, you're missing a trick.

Unions operate a membership structure with union leaders and delegates whose role is to represent their members, go to bat for them over pay and conditions, and keep them informed of what's happening in the organisation and in the wider world that is important to them. It's usually an efficient, active and regular set of activities and comms channels, including meetings, newsletters and noticeboards. Union officials and communicators have a very precise sense of what needs to be communicated to (and from) their members, and as an example of good internal comms, union communications with their members often has much to be admired.

But unions do often have a deep mistrust of management and what they communicate – for reasons I've identified elsewhere in this book: failure to communicate or to communicate openly and honestly. Union-management relations historically have been very rocky in many organisations, and co-operation in the area of comms can be a victim of that.

But corporate internal communicators should be working closely with their union counterparts, especially at times of significant change affecting workers. I'd urge you to do whatever you can to build bridges and establish mutual respect with your union representatives, involve them in the communications planning where it involves their membership and work with them and their channels to reach the unionised workforce.

5.3 COASTWATCHERS

Coastwatchers. Heard of them? They were the unsung heroes of World War 2, hidden away on Pacific islands spying on the Japanese and feeding information back to the Allies. Many were caught and executed but the work they did was often vital to the success of the Allies in combating Japan's military movements.

The coastwatchers metaphor has application in internal comms, without (I hasten to add) the threat of a large sword hanging over your head should you get caught doing it.

Where organisations have offices, branches, departments or worksites scattered across the land, Head Office-based comms people can't hope to know about everything that's going on. Even the local managers can miss things. But in each satellite place there are employees who do see, hear and experience important and interesting organisational activity that HO might have missed.

They may not be great or even good writers – they rarely are – but they're passionate, they're on the spot, and if they're encouraged and guided, they can get better at it. In my experience, such people like to be involved and appreciate seeing the fruits of their work appear in print. Internal Comms should foster such people; to tip you off on stories at the very least, but also maybe to pen an account for you, take or find a photo, or confirm details. They also provide important local validation of stories; writing from afar brings a real risk of missing details or focusing or angling the story wrong.

Coastwatchers reduce the risk significantly. Gold.

But there's another important side to coastwatchers. Too often comms teams produce materials like newsletter articles and recoil at any criticism about content or delivery. Email provides that feedback loop and it's foolish to ignore it.

The critique may be bookish and grammatical – and possibly wrong. Styles of delivery vary; who's right? Having a style guide in place gives you an authoritative rock to anchor your writings to. The *Economist* style guide (see Bibliography) is one of the best but there are others. More often than not, when colleagues complain about comms errors, they're probably right. Oops. You missed the typo' on page 11 – or got the spelling of Alistair/Alastair/Alasdair wrong (always check names).

Their critique may be grumpy too: they've spotted errors and it bugs them. You shouldn't be so sloppy. They're right again. If you're loose with the style, grammar and punctuation, how do we know you're not loose with the facts? And worse still - loose with your planning and organisation.

The important thing is that it's all well-intentioned. It's not meant to bait you. So you should embrace it; accept the response, apologise, thank them for it, learn from it...and don't make that error (if it is one) again. Take it on the chin with good grace and move on. If it's *your* blue.

If they're wrong, gently but firmly tell them.

Such correspondents are an editorial safety net of sorts. They read what you send intently so are obviously interested in the business. They can be more than your *ex post facto* proof-readers; view them through a positive lens – what do they see that you could, or should, communicate, and what do they think in general of your comms? It's not a stretch to foster them as an informal focus group on how comms is going.

It's also true that large documents like newsletters and booklets have to be human. They're never going to be perfect, and sometimes they need to be produced quickly, so errors occur. You're not *Cirque du Soleil* who give us slick, captivating, beautiful, wonderful spectacles built on years of work and huge resources. Internal comms isn't that sort of game. It's simpler and grittier. It can't look like a lot of money – flashy and opulent. It needs to be human and humble. It should tolerate the odd "sandfly in the finish coat" as the small-town surfboard-maker might say. It should be real.

People also dislike "spin" – tell it like it is. Quickly and well.

Colleagues who get to know you and what you do and respect both are also on your team really. They provide content and critique. They are closer to the action. They are an asset to internal comms. Welcome them. Educate them. Give them by-lines in newsletters. Build your team.

5.4 THE FOREIGN MASTER

Internal comms becomes more complex and interesting when your organisation is a multi-national one.

Especially so if your Head Office is in another country. That's a relatively common experience for NZ comms people: HO is in Australia or possibly Europe, the US, Asia.

Your lines of instruction may be extended and tenuous. HO control may be tight and stringent; or you could be relatively autonomous. Both have their pros and cons. The difficulty arises from the cultural differences between your organisation in its foreign location and your branch of the business. Global comms directions around some internal development might not quite fit the local scene. You have to adapt them. You may get very little steer at all. Global planning doesn't always specify how to apply the new initiative to your unique, far-flung (if it's New Zealand) patch. You have to figure it out. And there are some significant cultural differences around preferred comms approaches.

It calls for diplomacy. Awareness of other time zones. Patience and tolerance.

From an internal comms perspective, it's handy to understand (from your audit) what global information your local team needs and wants. It may be a narrow set of what's available simply because your country market is smaller and legislatively different in some important ways.

Global comms resources can be incredibly rich in all senses of the word. Your major, English-speaking, sister jurisdictions – the US and UK for example – may have troves of stuff you can use, including plans, case studies, templates, presentations, backgrounders. Tap into it; identify your counterparts at these places and make contact. Share and they'll share with you. But be aware: the global resources may *look* great, but you still need to scrutinise them carefully for both accuracy and local relevance and authenticity.

Though they may view you as a distant comms cousin in (in New Zealand's case) a quaint, remote backwater, your multi-national comms colleagues are also part of your team – and are generally well disposed to assist you. Talk with them too.

In Practice #3 - The A to Z

Everyone gets the alphabet. Handy device, shall we say. Here's a good internal comms use for that ready familiarity. Any time you have a body of information with lots of definitions or entities you want to make more widely known, turn it into an A-to-Z. But make it fun if you can.

This is a good way to compile corporate information about your operations; easy to search and can be electronically linked to more detailed files.

I did one for risk management (believe it or not) and made it into a poster. Sample definitions:

- G is for God. There are Acts of God and you can Trust in God, but you still need a Risk Management Plan…

- V is for Variety. One control may not be enough to keep the lid on a risk...a variety of controls gives greater protection.
- X is for xpense, xasperation, xhaustion and xplosions – things we avoid with xcellent risk control strategies.

Cut-through. Be different if you can.

CHAPTER 6

This section's for you*

With apologies to Neil Young

A s a communications person you quickly get into the habit of talking about your audiences – your publics, your stakeholders…call them what you like. Internal comms tends to lump them all under one heading – employees.

But as we've already explored, there are many shades of difference within the employed ranks of a business or organisation arising from differences in roles, ranking, location, hours worked (part or full time), temporary or permanent status and so on.

Another way to approach your stakeholders within an organisation is to identify who your "clients" are: who is issuing you with the briefs and instructions to go forth and communicate? It starts at, or near, the top.

6.1 CORPORATE OFFICE

Unquestionably, the corporate office – the CEO and the senior management team – looks to the internal comms team for employee comms. A large part of this book focuses on their comms needs, but there are some specific areas that we should single out to look at. One that grows in importance as society gets (we hope) progressively more enlightened is what has come to be known as Corporate Social Responsibility (CSR). This is increasing seen in Annual Reports that cover the "triple bottom line" – economic, social and environmental performance, the emergence of Sustainability Reports and the more recent arrival of Integrated Reports (capturing the triple bottom line in relation to the financials).

Corporates are doing more good works in the social area (which takes in wellness as well as how the organisation interfaces with society in a positive way) as well as the environment – noting their impacts and remedying where possible any adverse ones.

Such good works enhance the organisation's reputation which contributes to its marketing success and attractiveness to potential employees, but it's also the right thing to do, putting aside the financial and recruitment benefits.

And a lot of organisations are doing great things for employees, their communities and the environment. This is not the book to go into huge detail there; we're here to talk about the internal comms of it – and there's a lot of that. Much of the good works does get promoted externally and well, but the Cinderella effect reaches into this space too – employees often hear little or late – something I talk more about in my chapter on internal comms and external comms later in this book.

Wellness activities aside (if they're present), most CSR action is outward-facing, involving community activities, environmental protection, sponsorships and the like. The best activities involve employees to the max: both in terms of devising and deciding what good works to do, and in terms of getting them involved in the actual doing.

Volunteering

That brings me to the phenomenon known as Volunteering, which has become a strong plank in many CSR programmes across the globe. Essentially, it's about employees doing good works for their communities, society, the less well-off...for free. It is a lovely concept and in practice often does make a valuable contribution.

But it can become too strongly hitched to its PR objectives. It shouldn't look like a tick-box exercise created simply to improve the company's reputation. It should come from the heart – hence the importance of employees being strongly involved in deciding what to get behind.

And as HR people will attest therein lies a dilemma. If you ask 1000 employees what sort of volunteering they'd like to do, you may get close to that many different answers – from planting trees to helping stray cats to singing for old people.

So, often, the powers-that-be (or a sub-committee of the wise) decide for the organisation. A cause is chosen and on a particular day – maybe it's called Volunteer Day - everyone dons their branded t-shirt and heads out to do the volunteering. If it doesn't rain and you get good numbers, it can be very successful – in terms of achieving the objective of planting the trees and getting some media attention.

But for the employees it can be somewhat less of a success.

Here's why.

- Many may not have strongly supported the chosen cause (or at least it wasn't what they would have chosen to volunteer to do).
- Of those, some attended and enjoyed the "day off" or accepted it was an okay thing to do, while others chose to stay at work (unless it was mandated they attend – and you can imagine how they felt about that).
- Some might have taken a "sickie", seeing it as a waste of time.
- Some employees may have had other commitments (leave, urgent assignments and so on), so missed the Volunteer Day altogether – and it may have been a cause they greatly supported.
- Management may have ordained that the Volunteer Day would be on a Saturday or Sunday, and there may have been good reasons for that – that's when the community initiative was happening, for example. Though the real reason might be that some of those in Finance (and Corporate) view the idea of employees taking a working day off to volunteer as a massive hit to productivity.

A system of volunteering that works for all employees or as many as possible – there will always be people for whom *nothing* works - isn't an easy thing to organise but one system worth considering is the concept of a *volunteering voucher*. Each employee gets an annual voucher for one day's volunteering during work time for a cause that's dear to *their* hearts. They can combine with other employees all doing the same thing.

They can decide *when* they will do it; and can accrue their vouchers perhaps over two or more years to enable a sustained effort for some cause. Or it can be two half-days.

It's not compulsory. But it will need to be subject to the cause being acceptable to the organisation. And there will need to be evidence of the activity actually taking place!

Takes a bit to manage you say. Sure. But if it's worth doing, it's worth doing properly – and mean something to all employees.

6.2 OTHER DEPARTMENTS

So Corporate has a big call on internal comms. But the instructions don't all come from the top office.

Your "clients" – where you should also be looking for business – are the heads of the functional units (departments, divisions, shared services) who run the business for the Boss.

They are the heads of HR, Finance, Information Technology, H&S, Legal, Operations, Manufacturing, Research & Development, and to a lesser extent (in terms of internal comms needs) Sales & Marketing, Procurement, and Supply Chain. Your organisation may not have specific units for all of these but certainly the first four should be top of your internal client list.

If the heads of those units are not working closely with you to communicate with employees around the key activities happening in their area, be concerned...be very concerned. Most often, fortunately, the managers of those units do understand the need and value of comms planning. But let's work through each one in turn to identify their common comms needs and ways to address them.

Human Resources

It stands to reason that Human Resources has perhaps the biggest stake in proper comms planning. Their role is to hire people when they're needed, move them on if that's necessary, and ensure they are looked after while they're on the payroll and adhere to organisational policies and values.

HR's comms needs are constant – and are heightened at times of change, upheaval or disruption, such as mergers, downsizings, shifts in location, moves to outsourcing of key roles and a host of other business events that involve (and distract) staff.

Business-as-usual requirements include the comms around on-boarding new employees, such as induction, communication of policies and organisational values (more on which below), learning and development activities such as training and performance reviews, and wellness activities – though the last-named can bounce around between HR and H&S.

HR will (or should) provide the greatest chunk of comms activity for the internal comms person, and the relationship will work best when, well before the beginning of the new calendar or financial year, the HR Manager and comms person sit down with HR's "business" plan for the year ahead and identify where comms planning is required.

The HR plan of activity should have a sub-section called communications under each prescribed, proposed area of activity. Simple as that. This would spell out who needs to be communicated with, when and on what. If it's known. If the detail isn't clear yet, the plan should identify when it will be – with a trigger date to get going on the comms preparations.

Yet, it often doesn't happen. Or happens piecemeal, or at the last minute. Internal comms should be meeting and talking with HR regularly; they are handmaidens within the organisation. HR doesn't work without robust employee comms planning and activities. As I detail in the next chapter on communicating change, at times of significant workplace disruption it's about communicating more, more regularly, face-to-face and with a strong emphasis on why the change is happening. That's the blueprint. You may be faced with massive organisational work to do and have a lean team – but don't skimp on the comms. It's crucial.

Most, if not all, organisations of any size will have the standard internal comms tools and channels operating, including an internal newsletter, an intranet perhaps and hopefully regular all-staff updates. HR should be close to all of them.

There's also plenty of scope for formal comms support for the organisation's onboarding programme. An induction day for groups of new staff is comms through-and-through and can be efficient, informative and fun – or dense, dull and dire. Miles of PowerPoint presentations and a surfeit of talking heads can be an overwhelming, flat introduction to the organisation. Good comms planning will help make it more palatable, manageable and understandable for attendees (and presenters).

Values

Within the HR orbit, one of the most problematic areas to communicate is values – a subset of culture.

The best definition of culture within an organisation to me is still "the way we do things around here", and values are the underlying principles and behaviours that underpin that. Values must be real - actual and evident. The other dimension organisations are increasingly focusing on in their values is the "why". Why we do things the way we do them.

Within an organisation, the enduring values are the ones that are second nature to everyone in the business – honesty, respect, diligence…whatever they are. The flaky ones are the ones that are claimed to exist but really don't – or aren't honoured by everyone.

Organisations are great at formulating a raft of values, maybe arrived at through a representative assembly of employees, that they believe should underpin life at the workplace. Posters are made, company presentations are given on the new values, emails fly out about them, people start getting recognised for showing the values. All good you might think; mission accomplished. But over time you start to realise that many of the values are purely aspirational – in some people's eyes. Actual behaviours within the organisation often don't reflect the values at all.

A classic one is a value typically called Openness, Honesty or Transparency. We know what that's about – communicating and communicating the truth. Few would disagree that it's an essential and important value within an organisation.

But what do the employee engagement surveys tell us time and again? Management aren't open with us, they're not honest about what's happening, there's no transparency. Your reputation as a manager or management team who can be trusted in this area takes a long time to build – and seconds to wreck in many employees' eyes through an act of obfuscation, brick-walling or apparent informational dishonesty.

The best values rise from what is observed as being "the way we do things around here", ie demonstrable and widely accepted and practised behaviours, as noted earlier.

Which is not to say organisations can't and shouldn't aspire to adopting and promoting new behaviours that are seen as a desirable development for the organisation. Just don't expect to be able to mandate that a new value will "now be practised by everyone". This is akin to that line someone quipped years back about "the beatings continuing till morale improves". No amount of fancy posters and presentations will make new values take root in an organisation if many employees don't "get" or support them. You need to be able to make the case for new behaviours/values to become part of the fabric of the organisation, and that calls for consultation, discussion, debate.

And management have to be scrupulous themselves in demonstrating the new values 24/7. That other old phrase "Do as we say – not as we do" comes to mind.

Some values are a challenge to bed down; others are more straightforward. Values around H&S everyone except the wantonly reckless (and deranged) will get, and while H&S procedures can be laborious and repetitive, there's near-universal acceptance of that line around "getting you home safely to your family at night."

More touchy-feely values take more work. But the more people who champion the values and demonstrate them, the more likely they are to flourish in time. Acknowledging people in the organisation who have demonstrated a value to a high level is good practice. But be wary of posting a monetary reward, especially a significant one, for great values behaviour. As Daniel Pink pointed out in his excellent book on motivation, *Drive: The Surprising Truth About What Motivates Us* (Riverhead, 2009), the incentive for demonstrating the value should be that it's intrinsically the right thing to do – monetary rewards change the motivation significantly[5].

A last word on values. Don't try to launch and sell a set of values when you're restructuring, particularly if there's the high probability of job changes or job losses through downsizing. Employees facing questions around whether they have a job and what's going to happen if they don't (or do, but it's a different job) don't have the mental space or aptitude to engage in discussing new behaviours. The very worst situation occurs when one of the new values is about Openness etc – and management keep the staff in the dark about what's happening. Ludicrous, but I've seen it happen. Wait till the restructuring is complete and you're taking stock of what the new organisation looks like – and what's important to it. And then maybe begin a discussion around "how we do things around here."

Wellness

Here's another HR mainstay: wellness. As noted earlier, in my experience the concept of wellness within an organisation can still be somewhat hazily defined, and "ownership" can be transient. HR might look after it; or it could reside with H&S. Or no one.

Organisations where HR has a strong hand in what I call "pastoral care", ie looking after employees, generally hold the wellness reins. But in some organisations, HR is very much more about recruitment and discipline – hiring and firing –

and pastoral care can seem a lesser priority. In such cases, wellness may end up with H&S as an offshoot of the health programme.

But H&S is also often very much about the hard end of their brief. Safety, especially in organisations exposed to operational dangers such as engineering companies, can be the dominant part of the action. Health will keep the team busy too; health checks, testing, flu jabs, diet and exercise maybe. Good organisations do great work in keeping their employees fit and healthy. There may be a gym onsite or gym membership perks.

Then there's wellness. Less about physical health and more about mental health. It's the domain of stress, burnout, depression, absenteeism, personal tragedy. How people are feeling about their work, their lives.

It's the hard one to address. Un-wellness (in the mental health sense) can arise from many things including workplace bullying or sexual harassment. It's often invisible; employees keep their mental wellbeing private – or share it with a very few close friends or colleagues.

Mass and group interventions – like vaccination programmes or Cardiovascular (CV) Risk Assessment campaigns - can't sort this stuff out. It takes careful interventions and individual counselling, and nothing will be remedied overnight.

Organisations with wellness programmes try to fence the cliff road rather than react when the problem is well advanced. The new breed of wellness programmes comes into play – Yoga classes, meditation rooms, mindfulness training. Happy staff, happy customers.

But many organisations feel it's enough to simply tell their staff about external providers, like the Employee Assistance

Programme (EAP), and are inclined to leave it up to the individuals to sort their own issues out – though a perceptive and caring manager usually gets more involved. Letting employees sort their own grief out feels like an abrogation of responsibility, particularly if it arises from workplace issues, and many problems risk going unresolved where the onus is on the individual to privately seek help.

One last point under the HR subheading: remember that organisations don't exist without people and their stories are gold, internally and externally. Where employees do well at work or at play, tell people about it. Tell their human stories in getting to their successes, but also just reflect their passion for the job, their interest in their industry, the contribution they make individually or as a team. Shine a light on them.

Finance

An organisation's bean counters and number-crunchers are a vital part of its operations. They monitor and manage its fiscal survival, and in businesses, they steward the company's revenue-making and profitability in tandem with the sales and marketing team. What care they about internal comms? Well, the truth is, a good deal of the time they aren't really too concerned about what information they need to get to staff. There's the standard stuff related to employees' pay, like annual announcements around pay rises (or when they're not going to happen), bonuses and other payroll-related information. They may also have news about share issues (if it's a listed company) or company-negotiated "perks" such as discounts at other businesses.

But wear the shoes of the employees and there's a very vital area of information they should be keeping staff informed about: how the organisation is doing. There's a perception that the workers out there just want to get on and do their jobs and don't really care too much about what the "suits" in Head Office are doing. But I think that's overstated. Some employees don't. But my impression is that most employees – blue- or white-collar – care deeply about how the organisation is doing for the very simple reason that if it's doing badly, their future employment is threatened.

So they want to hear about the organisation's directions, its business plans, its intentions to move into new areas of revenue or out of old ones. They want to be reassured that the business is doing well – or if it's not, what that means: what the organisation is going to do about it and how can *they* – the employees - help keep the place viable and prosperous.

But typically, the angst about the organisation's fiscal and business situation gets held tightly under wraps and employees only learn about it when the drastic action is about to take place.

Organisational updates, whatever the frequency (and they should be at least every couple of months if not more frequently at times of significant change or challenge), should feature some kind of report card from the Finance team about "how we're doing". A review of the previous period; a look-forward to the period ahead – key activities, goals and challenges. What needs to happen and how the organisation proposes to make it happen, to stay viable and hopefully prosperous.

Finance also has a big stake in the culminative period of the financial year, when the annual result is announced. The internal announcement of this is a key "state of the nation" event and should capture and present to employees the highs and lows, the wins, gains and losses, the lessons learnt, as well as presenting a vision of where the organisation is headed in the next 12 months. Much of this gets the full comms department treatment for external audiences, where the business is public – half-yearly reports, annual reports, integrated reports, sustainability reports and the like get meticulously prepared, consuming large resources of comms time and money, but invariably, telling the internal audience is almost an after-thought. Many employees "read it in the paper." Not good.

Make a plan and capture all of the above in it, Mr/Ms CFO.

Information Technology

In the digital era, the Information Technology (IT) department (often known as the Computer and Information Technologies – CIT department) carries a huge burden of keeping everyone connected and resourced to do their jobs. Their asset base is huge: cellphones, laptops, tablets, desktop PCs, servers, networks, software, video-conferencing rooms – a vast assemblage of kit that needs maintenance, repair and probably regular upgrading or replacement.

The IT team probably has a workable system of managing the business-as-usual interaction with their internal clients, but occasionally they have a more substantial information challenge like a large rollout of new kit, a move to a new software platform or a structural change such as a move to outsourcing a part of what they do (which brings the double whammy of organisational disruption *and* potential job losses).

Any of those will cry out for solid internal comms planning and implementation, possibly over a long period of time: announcements (including explanations of the rationale for what's happening); timetables; training programmes; and consultation processes (in conjunction with HR) if there's an outsourcing or team downsizing. Make a Plan, Mr/Ms CIO.

Health & Safety

H&S is another department that will have a lot to gain from a close working relationship with internal comms.

H&S has high priority in most if not all good organisations simply because it's literally in many cases a "do-or-die" thing. A fall down three stairs can leave an employee seriously injured and off work for many months; a moment's inattention in the field can lead to a fatal event. The stakes are high where safety is concerned, and H&S departments have a lot to have to manage, monitor, track and report on.

Legislation sets the bar and the punishment for inadvertently and carelessly allowing your employees to get hurt is quite severe now. In response, organisations put in place policies and practices to essentially remove the room for error within the system. Human error was usually blamed in the past for accidents and humans still make errors and will continue to (it's human nature), but current thinking is to get the systems working properly to the point where human error won't lead to a tragedy.

H&S will have policies in place or new ones being launched and internal comms has a place in announcing the new ones (what it involves and the rationale) and providing reminders re the standing ones. H&S also sets targets for accident reduction and there's regular scope to advise employees on how they're doing against those targets.

When accidents occur, employees need to be advised and lessons noted, along with what's being done to avoid the same happening again.

As an aside, I'm not a fan of the tendency to track the hours without a Lost-Time Injury (LTI) occurring; it's such a downer when, after a long injury-free period, one occurs. It brings a sudden, unnecessarily gloomy vibe to the workplace, when the organisation should be reflecting on the low percentage of accidents over a long period of time. Instead there's this sense of failure, and of having to start again at the bottom.

H&S, like Finance and HR, should be grabbing a spot at each company update to tell their story – reflecting on what's happened and the lessons arising, and the good work that's taking place.

Like safety, there's plenty to talk about in the health area too. Again, it's about policies and procedures to keep people well at work. It can be controversial: encouraging better eating habits, moderation in drinking, vaccination against disease, smoking cessation, and avoidance of drugs – controversial because many people don't like being told what's good for them. Internal Comms has a role to support H&S in informing staff about the health issues, the rationale for the policies and how the organisation proposes to address them.

Many organisations are active in the health area, running health checks, CV risk assessments, eyesight testing, diet clinics and so on. Some set aside considerable time and money to hold a Health & Safety week (or even month) with multiple presentations and external speakers. I'm a big fan of that (see the example at the end of this chapter). I can't see the point of a Health & Safety Day – blink and you'll miss it.

But having health and safety the dominant points of conversation for an extended period makes sense to me.

If that happens, as an internal comms person, expect (nay, demand) to be involved. It takes a lot of planning and selling, and comms is a key part of the action.

Those are the main internal "clients" for the internal comms person to service. But other aspects of the organisation will have a call on internal comms from time to time.

Other departments

An Internal Comms Manager should be on affable speaking terms with the managers of all departments. The following are less reliant on large amounts of internal comms action but should still be on your radar:

- **Sales and Marketing**. You market and sell externally, but every employee should know about the beauty of your products or services (and not just through "reading it in the paper"). Keep them informed about what you make or do and why it's so good; non-sales employees are really an informal extension of your salesforce. Let them know how you're doing in terms of sales, new product development and so on; remember – they're (usually) vitally interested in the success of the organisation.

- **Manufacturing and Distribution**. There are stories to tell out of manufacturing: new processes, great ideas, new efficiencies, new machinery, new lines. Ditto distribution; how the product gets out there is a story worth illuminating too, with innovation, ingenuity, and commitment occurring but often going unrecognised internally.

- **Procurement and Supply Chain**. Yet another set of cogs within the organisation that may go unheralded. Herald them.

6.3 THE IDEAS FACTORY

Organisations experience challenges every day. Across a raft of processes and functions to achieve the organisation's goals things can go wrong or can appear wasteful or inefficient.

There is scope to seek out and implement better ways to do things or to save money, time or other resources. For many (if not most) organisations, chasing efficiencies and greater productivity are an ongoing mantra.

A common approach to getting better processes is to haul in an external consultant (or a team of them) to independently review what's happening and suggest improvements – and perhaps do the work to implement them. A good deal of the time this is an effective approach, because their skills are not strongly represented in the workplace and they bring a fresh, independent perspective.

But there's an external wariness of consultants for a number of reasons. They often arrive unannounced and with their reason for being onsite unknown to many. Suspicion kicks in; perhaps they're here to (gulp) downsize the organisation. And besides, what do they really know about our business?

But a large portion of the resistance comes from the fact that the process often bypasses and ignores the experience of the people at the coalface. They know the operations intimately and do have ideas about how to improve things but rarely get a chance to unveil them.

So productivity and efficiency are things that get done *to* them, rather than something they have a hand in doing. The best organisations listen to their frontline employees, or better still have a formal and regular mechanism for inviting their suggestions on how to improve things. That's an important first step.

But the organisation also has to see the promise through: too often the idea heads up the chain and stalls somewhere in the middle – and nothing happens. Suggestion boxes are a common approach to try to "automate" the idea-gathering process but we all know of places where it was clear to staff that no one, after a time, even emptied the boxes. Lip service.

No, you must commit to the concept of farming the best ideas of your employees. Receiving and processing them properly, seeing them through to fruition and acknowledging the originators. Do you reward them? Perhaps – but refer to my earlier comments re intrinsic versus monetary motivations (Daniel Pink's thesis). Recognition of your contribution by peers and managers is a powerful motivator.

In Practice # 4 – "March for Safety"

It's an adage followed faithfully over the years by advertising: *Dominate the airwaves…* if you really want your messages to have some impact.

But we tend to set aside a single day for things: Volunteering Day, Health & Safety Day, Diversity Day. But blink…and it's gone.

Try a month of focus – *March 4 Safety* (held in March but a pun intended…*Safebruary* was another option) - as we did, for a large technology company with three major sites and a strong blue-collar/white-collar split. Health, Safety and Environment activities for a month; not all-day/everyday, of course, but a rich programme of speakers, demonstrations, workshops and discussions. A lot at lunchtimes; attend what you like when you can. Include safety at home.

Not overly expensive; many speakers were happy to give up time for the cause.

Organise it like you mean it. Enable everyone to have a slice of the action. Make it memorable.

Channelling Russian propaganda posters...the A1 poster for March 4 Safety (Design – Steve Turner, Toast Design 2009)

CHAPTER 7

Comms in times of change

*The first step towards change is awareness.
The second step is acceptance. – **Nathaniel
Branden***

*People don't resist change. They resist being
changed. – **Peter Senge***

For the internal comms practitioner, managing the comms around change used to be an occasional task or project.

Not anymore it seems. Organisations striving to stay viable, functional and/or relevant have to confront the need for change pretty much constantly.

It's often personnel-based: shifts in the organisation's people resource brought on by whatever external or internal winds are raging. That may be shifts in the market or the world we do our business in. Or it's technical and operational: we change the way we do things, bring in new things.

Something changes, and we have to change in line with it. But as is only human nature, many people don't like change. It means uncertainties. Confidence in what you're doing and have done for a long time is eroded by the threat of change. You don't want it to happen. Can't we avoid it?

If not managed carefully, change invariably brings resistance. Motivation falls. Productivity falls. Morale falls. Some change is unnecessary. It's an over-reaction. A knee-jerk. You hope the organisation (or its masters at the top) don't make this error.

But most change is unavoidable. It's going to happen sooner or later (better sooner). It must happen.

How should it happen?

Imagine a clock – and for this metaphor I'm indebted to one of the great commentators on this change business, Rick Maurer, whose excellent book on resistance to change (and how to address it, including change communications) *Beyond the Wall of Resistance: Why 70% of All Changes Still Fail – and What You Can Do About It* (Bard Press, 2010) I heartily recommend. I've adapted Maurer's cycle of change[6] somewhat for this discussion but hopefully the principle is still the same.

Let's imagine we're at 12 on the clock and it becomes clear to us as a senior management team that we need to make some changes to our business or we're in deep doodoo. We assess the problem – what's really wrong here? At about 1pm (metaphorically speaking) we agree among ourselves that it's bad and we need to change something or things. We formulate some options…3pm. We debate these and decide what the best option is…4pm. We work out how we would implement the chosen option…5pm. Then we proceed to roll it out…6pm.

And all hell breaks loose.

People are shocked. Upset. How can you do that? We don't like it. We don't want it. Make it go away!

The problem? You and your senior colleagues who held the discussions, made the decisions, came up with the solution, and rolled it out, are at 7 o'clock. But just about everyone else is still at 12 – they don't even see what's wrong. It hasn't been explained to them. They thought we were doing OK.

You didn't take them with you on the journey.

Bill Quirke[7] depicts this another way: a funnel and a pyramid overlaying each other. The pyramid - narrow at top, wide at bottom – represents the involvement process, ie a few people at the start of discussions (the top of the pyramid) and everyone at the end (the base) when you're rolling out your solution. The right-way-up funnel represents the process of reviewing objectives, exploring needs and considering options (at the top), evaluating them – when you've narrowed the field of possibilities, and announcing the conclusions and the chosen option – the narrow bit of the funnel.

Get the picture? You've brought everyone in when there's nothing to discuss or decide. It's a *fait accompli.*

This is not rocket science and there is often an attempt to make this change process consultative, but it can be a bit of a sham. Options are laid out but there's often one that's already been covertly ordained as the winner. To be fair it's often the best or right one, but the process still evokes a sense of cynicism – you've decided already and you're just going through the façade of consulting with us. True debate about the options hasn't occurred.

But the critical stroke is a step earlier than that. It's the expression of the compelling rationale for the change. The *why*. If you haven't made the case strongly for change to happen, you won't get buy-in to the process of working out what to do to fix the problem. You'll get resistance.

Internal comms person – this is where you must thump the big table. Has the need for change been raised, discussed, and agreed broadly? You have to make that happen. Your senior managers lead this discussion; it is face-to-face and robust. It isn't an open-ended process in terms of time – we don't have the luxury of endless time to solve the problem because the worse it gets, the harder it will be to remedy. We make it democratic, but we make it very clear that, for good reasons, doing nothing (status quo-ing) is not an option.

Practically, this is about the three-part formula[8] which forms the crux of the excellent book on change communications by Larkin and Larkin:

- **communicate directly to supervisors** – involving them first to help them understand and share the messages with their teams
- **use face-to-face communications**
- **communicate relative performance of the local work area** - and link the change to the future prosperity and survival of the organisation – providing the compelling rationale for it (if there is one – if there isn't, oh dear).

The moment change comes on the agenda, it's human nature that almost all employees shrink their working focus to four questions:

- Will I still have a job?
- If I do, will it be the same as my old job?
- If it's different, will I be given training and support to do it properly?
- If I don't have a job, will the organisation look after me?

Communicating the rationale for change is the Internal Comms Manager's first and biggest task in a change situation.

Do that well, and there is generally a well-established HR guidebook to how change should be rolled out with personnel. It's underpinned by law and the proper, respectful treatment of employees. Comms supports the preparation of information that will be provided to managers and employees – the consultation documents, the emails, the presentations... whatever tools and channels are needed to inform the organisation of what's happening.

There are more face-to-face events than normal, they are more regular, and they allow plenty of two-way flow.

The internal comms person is also there to ensure management doesn't drop the ball. Nobody likes bad news, but it happens, and if there is a rational explanation for what has happened – it was necessary and unavoidable – in time people will accept it and move on.

But bad news *delivered badly* scores badly with the punters. That's what they remember.

So you never lie. You don't make the mistake of not telling them *anything* because you can't tell them *everything*. You tell them what you do know, and what as yet you don't have the answers to...with some indication (as best you can estimate it) of when you will have that missing information. And promise you'll tell them then. Then keep your promise.

And you front. Top leadership needs to speak. If you hide, it suggests you have something to hide.

I recall a brave health sector manager fronting a rural New Zealand community about the impending closure of their hospital. He addressed them on the reasons and got a hostile response, but earned their respect for fronting. Bad news, sure – but delivered in person.

In Practice # 5 - Transformation

Your organisation is being dramatically restructured for essentially political reasons. There will be job losses. It's a tense time.

You organise a regular set of updates – each with a different food theme. You call it the Katchup. A carpenter makes you a 1.5m sandwich board shaped like a tomato sauce bottle, which goes up outside the meeting room.

Rumours about what's going happen are rife. You write the worst rumours on balloons – and the CEO pops them at the Katchups.

Corny? You bet. Memorable. Yes.

CHAPTER 8

Internal communications and external communications

*Mushroom Management: where employees are kept in the dark and periodically fed a load of horse manure. - **Unknown***

As noted earlier, comms departments vary in number of staff in line with the size or complexity of the organisation and the business it needs to be communicating about – as a rule.

Internal and external comms are often akin to Cinders and her sisters – leading quite separate lives.

The rough definition has external comms encompassing all those groups of people who matter to your business – who have a stake in what it does (hence the popular term - stakeholders) except your employees. In no particular order of importance, those external audiences/stakeholders are:

- **customers** (other businesses if you're B2B, or consumers)
- the **Government** and government organisations
- the **community**, particularly if your business affects them directly
- strategic **partners** in your industry or sector
- **influencers** in your industry or sector
- the **media** including commentators and "bloggers".

External comms covers the work done to talk to those groups, and can usefully be divided into:

- **marketing communications**, which covers Public Relations, advertising, direct marketing, digital and social media and other promotional disciplines related to selling your goods and services or ideas
- **corporate communications**, which is more concerned with corporate image and reputation, issues and crisis management, government relations, investor relations, community relations, corporate social responsibility and other non-marketing matters.

Healthy external comms calls for solid planning and strategy across all those stakeholders; nothing is neglected and nothing left to chance.

But that shouldn't be at the expense of your employees. Unfortunately, it often is.

Managers (and Board members) never like to "read about it in the papers", that is, learn something about their organisation they didn't know – particularly something negative, from a reporter's story. So there's generally a lot of diligence about making sure that doesn't happen to the team at the top.

But it's a regular occurrence for many employees outside the senior management team. And there's nothing quite as embarrassing as being told about something concerning your organisation by your neighbour, who heard it on the radio, when you haven't the foggiest idea what they're talking about.

With any development of importance involving the organisation, particularly where it concerns the future of their workplace, employees should be among the first to hear about it – and certainly before the organisation goes public with it. A healthy internal comms programme would ensure that happens.

Employees usually *do* like to "read about it in the paper", if it's not a surprise. If it's good news, it's a source of pride in their organisation and reassurance that they have a secure working future. If it's bad news, and they've been sensitively informed about it before it hits the streets, they'll accept the exposure. If it's criticism of the organisation, they'll take pride in an honest and timely response from management that defends the issue well. If management doesn't do so, if it ducks and dives, hides from the media or blames them or anyone else for something that was clearly the organisation's fault...well, shame.

That's the game you play. You can't separate your employees from external communications because the moment they leave the office or factory gates, they are "external" and may encounter your external messaging.

More importantly, they are an army of external communicators in their own right – a point often forgotten by management. They talk about their work to friends and family; they Facebook and Twitter and email and text and if they're stirred up about some work matter it will come out in their personal, private – but sometimes very public –

conversations. They get asked regularly "How's work?" What they answer is often heavily coloured by how well they feel the organisation treats them. What would you like them to say? What would help them say it?

At the core of most work dissatisfaction and disengagement, as examination of just about any employee engagement survey will attest, is communication – or lack of it. Engagement surveys of the "net promoter" type are a fair gauge of employees' satisfaction or otherwise with their employer and place of work. Not a perfect gauge, not least because they're a rare (and anonymous) opportunity for employees to "vent", so the comments aren't always objective or fair. But they're a reasonable barometer of how things actually are.

Those who bother to reply and add comments often cite poor comms as an organisational failing that affects their engagement. Comms teams often groan at that revelation; what they usually mean is "my manager (or senior management) doesn't communicate with me". The provision of a general comment around "poor communications" is of almost no help to a Comms Manager trying to figure out how to improve things. What do they mean? Only a more focused internal comms audit can enable you to drill down to where the real failings and disconnections are.

So the lesson is: if you are going to communicate something publicly, make sure employees are told first. But also be aware that the moment you do inform staff, it is a 140-character tweet away from being public anyway, so your external comms on the same matter needs to be poised to hit the airwaves very soon after.

In some workplaces this is an issue. Where management and employees, generally in the shape of the workplace unions, don't have a good working relationship, news can leak. That's an unfortunate symptom of something deep-seated affecting the workers' relationship with their employers, which is beyond the scope of this book to discuss. But in my experience poor comms is often part of the malaise.

But returning to the "telling staff first" strategy. How do you do that?

Go back to your channels. If you have planned this piece of comms well, you'll have worked out your "story" – the key messages – and which stakeholders it needs to be told to, including employees.

Your comms team should then "slice and dice" the story to suit the various audiences.

If you take it to your employees face-to-face, it's in the presentation, the words of the CEO or the line manager, and the Q&A session. There's a follow-up email, a story in the internal newsletter, and something on the intranet. It may be on the noticeboard, or in the next corporate video.

It's a **360-degree approach**: lots of exposure in the hope at least one channel will get to every employee. And here's something to remember: it's a strange foible, but some (a very small number) of employees don't give a hoot. They will studiously, diligently and energetically *avoid* being communicated with, or to. They delete your emails without reading them, they shun the important meetings, they never ask questions. Phantom-like, they turn up, do their job, and go home without a great deal of engagement in the wider issues. They don't really care and don't want to know. But when things do turn pear-shaped, they're often among the first to complain. For obvious reasons.

There is a tendency too to think that frontline, blue-collar workers aren't really interested in all that Head-Office, management-speak mumbo-jumbo. And it's true they don't generally want to be earbashed about bureaucratic rigmarole. But they will usually be vitally interested in how the company is doing, and reassurances that management aren't screwing it up. Their livelihoods depend on it.

Once employees have had the opportunity to hear the news and understand it, your external channels can swing into action. A media release perhaps, a letter to suppliers and strategic partners, a website story, social media posts, a magazine interview or article.

Hopefully, your well-informed employees can embellish with good supportive comments the external conversations about what's happened or happening to the organisation that then take place. That's the ideal anyway, and in some organisations, it happens.

CHAPTER 9

Communicating with your partners

Clearly, employees are your primary internal audience. But there are other stakeholders who form part of an organisation's "extended family"; they are the people in other organisations who aren't full- or part-time employees but who contribute to what your organisation does.

They are your partners, though generally not in the legal sense of the word. In no particular order of importance, they include:

- **distributors**
- **suppliers** (of services, raw materials)
- external **consultants** and **advisers** (including Legal, HR and PR/Marketing/Communications)
- **contract manufacturers**
- organisations you **sponsor**.

They may have a long-standing arrangement with your organisation, and have become an integral cog in achieving your organisational goals. By being involved in your business or operations they have a stake in how successful or not you are – just like your employees. So keeping them informed of changes or developments in your business or operations that might affect *their* business is important.

They also don't like "reading about it in the paper"; they appreciate and respect any efforts to keep them apprised of what (and how) the company/organisation is doing. That doesn't, of course, mean sharing sensitive or confidential information about your organisation's plans or issues.

But there is a body of information that you can share, and doing so is important to the relationship you have with your partners.

And don't forget to *listen* to them. They may know your business or operations almost as well as you and can bring valuable business intelligence around the market or political developments, as well as advocating for you to the wider world. They're an asset and an ally, able to add value beyond the simple transactional arrangement you may have with them.

9.1 CHANNELS

So what does that body of partner comms look like?

Your written agreements with your partners *should* capture how both parties will communicate with each other, when and on what – but often don't get into that detail.

Gold standard is to meet with your partners individually at some point in the financial or planning year. The agenda will vary, but a face-to-face meeting provides an opportunity to catch up on any key organisational, marketing or personnel changes that have happened or are going to happen. It also does wonders for the relationship to actually meet rather than transact the relationship by remote control through letters and emails. The context of the meeting is the business relationship you have; under discussion is how it is going, can be improved, may change and so on.

There is a place for written comms, of course; you can't necessarily meet every time you have some news or something to discuss. So there's a space for occasional email updates from the relevant manager. The CEO's signature at the bottom also carries a lot of impact.

Your message essentially to your partners is that you value their contribution – if indeed you do, and if you don't that's a separate area of comms – and want to keep them in the loop around important developments occurring.

Other comms options are to include them in the distribution of your internal (and external) newsletters, invite them to organisational updates or offer to meet with and address their employees.

Is there a risk? Only if what is shared in the newsletters or updates is commercially sensitive or relates to change that you need to share with your employees only (at least initially).

It's worth noting that internal newsletters can't be kept confidential; the moment they're released they can be shared with anyone on the planet. Similarly, content delivered at an update can be transmitted wider afield by word-of-mouth. You have very little control over that.

Your partners should definitely be part of your comms planning at times of major change though, since they may be markedly affected.

If change is looming, you need to assess the impact of it on them and plan to raise it with them, inform them and discuss it accordingly – before the media beats you to it.

CHAPTER 10

Measuring and evaluating success

L et's assume your company masters have given you, the Internal Comms Manager, the latitude to plan and implement good comms programmes for staff – whether it's business as usual or a change phase.

Sooner or later someone will ask: Did it work? Or, even more ominously: What's the return on investment (ROI)?

It's absolutely right and sensible to try to measure and evaluate whether the comms has been successful. But how do you effectively measure it?

Internally, there are many surrogate measures of whether a piece of comms you have completed has had the desired effect. Firstly (and most obviously): employees do what the comms required them to do. They are not confused about what's going on; their managers report they all understand and accept it (as reflected in feedback at meetings and during their daily work). There are no disruptions to business processes through uncertainty, lack or shortage of information or employee resistance because they don't accept what's changing.

But Internal Comms Managers and their bosses also have other tools that can reveal the success or otherwise of internal comms activities:

- employee engagement surveys
- internal comms audits
- more focused surveys
- focus groups.

10.1 EMPLOYEE ENGAGEMENT SURVEYS

Engagement surveys, as noted earlier in this book, are of limited use to communicators trying to measure the effectiveness of their work. Their scope is much broader than simply comms; and what comms insights they produce are usually very general – giving a broad thumbs-down or thumbs-up to the function, as an aspect of what motivates people to stay with the organisation (or leave), without really revealing the detail you need to be able to act.

They do give you a signal that, in general terms, comms is okay (or the reverse), but you get better information from the other tools.

10.2 INTERNAL COMMUNICATIONS AUDITS

Assuming you've carried out a benchmark internal comms audit (Chapter 2), which has shown what works and what doesn't – and what you need to work on – you will get strong insights into how well your comms has gone when you carry out subsequent repeat audits.

You need to allow time for the remedial or supplementary comms work to take effect. But once a reasonable time has elapsed for the changes you've made to bear fruit, you should re-audit employees with a very similar (if not identical) set of audit questions to the first one you did. Timing is probably around a year later but it could well be six months, depending on how hard-out you go to implement changes to your internal comms programmes, practices, policies, channels and tools. Comparing the two sets of data will tell you if there's been growth or improvement.

10.3 MORE-FOCUSED SURVEYS

If you are seeking to measure the growth in awareness and understanding around some specific aspect of the business among staff, one time-honoured way is to survey them on it. That may be a new H&S initiative or policy, for example. Ask them what they know, ask them if they understand, ask them what they haven't yet grasped. Managers can do the same with their teams; it may simply be that sort of verbal canvassing at a meeting. That does take discipline and the buy-in from managers to make the effort – but if you're wanting to know if employees understand something, what better way than to simply ask them? We don't do enough of that.

10.4 FOCUS GROUPS

Focus groups are a mainstay of research organisations, but it doesn't need a research organisation to set one up inside an organisation. If you want to understand whether a comms programme has been effective, gather a representative sample of employees who were exposed to it and *ask them how it went.*

If you were *really* organised, you'd have a standing group that provided you with regular feedback, especially through an extended period of change when the comms escalates in importance and urgency. Why not?

Cinderella revisited

So there you have it. The internal comms world according to me. I'm certainly not the first person to write on the subject and other commentators and instructors will take the topic places I can't, as time – and the way we communicate - moves on. You may not agree with everything I posit here, and this is just one man's experience, so I'm sure there are "sandflies in the finish coat" of my overall thesis.

But I would fight hard for the fact that internal comms can be done better – and often much, *much* better. That I'm pretty certain of; I've had very few people tell me their Internal Comms is fantastic, though when things go well, most employees are charitable enough to actually commend you. Things turned to pumpkin for Cinders at midnight. But she *did* get the prince in the end.

While writing and producing this book – an undertaking that proved more laborious that I originally thought – I was often asked: Who was it for? I originally thought it was for my fellow comms professionals or people starting out or training in the comms game. Then I extended that to any manager in an organisation, from the top down. But as time wore on I realised it was relevant to ANY employee in an organisation remotely interested in what was going on around them at work. Regardless of whether they manage communications – I thought this book might be something of a guide to how those who *do* manage comms could perhaps do it better. So non-comms people can gently support change for the better.

If you, the reader, *do* manage comms in your organisation – or manage the organisation itself – there is one simple rule that I would carve into the lintel above the door. And it's contained in the very first words of this book: Talk with your people.

About.

Everything.

ACKNOWLEDGEMENTS

Thanks

I would like to thank the following wonderful people for helping me get this book out of my head (and my heart) and onto paper, press and the digital highway.

My wife Jill and sons Cam and Duncx who tolerated the old duffer disappearing into the study to write, aware that it was a labour largely of love and unlikely to make us all a fortune.

Cam too for the cover concept he designed for this book and Jonathan Templeman of Design Dairy for helping get the book to a finished state.

My close friends and colleagues who, hearing I was grinding out an internal comms book, were encouraging and supportive: Clare Feeney, Rob Bialostocki and Therese Kelly, William Malpass, Donald Bowie, Greg Ward, Alexa Langdale, Tim Marshall, my yum-char crew - Stephen McDonald and Chris Ryan, Andrew and Miriam Ferguson, Shirley Johnston, Sandra Kanny, Carlos Humphris, Tony and Yvonne Coburn, Melanie McKay, and my boss at Wright Communications, Nikki Wright.

Clare, Tim and Melanie for patiently hunting the typos and gently querying the curiosities of expression and other excesses in the manuscript.

Awesome people with much greater experience and knowledge of the publishing game who gave me valuable advice and encouragement: Geoff Chapple, Martin Taylor, Graham Reid and Roger Horrocks.

My bosses from the past who tolerated and took a punt on the eccentricities and occasional stubbornness of their Comms Manager: Chris Mules and Hugh Kininmonth at Midland RHA, Fran Percy and Dave Clarke at South Auckland Health and the Counties-Manukau DHB, Michael Bryant and Ian Griffiths at GSK, Phil Johnstone and Mark Vanderwee at MSD, Paul Ravlich at Siemens, and Jenni Austin and Peter Reidy at KiwiRail.

And finally, the wise people who guided my first foray into PR: Pauline Rose, Tony Farrington, Peter Debreceny and Tony Neilson; and two gents who also taught me much - my brilliant English HOD at Rangitoto College Brian Lamb and my ATI journalism tutor, the late Geoff Black. They all had a hand in shaping the practitioner (and person) I am, and I'm grateful for the time I had, to learn from them.

Terima kasih banyak.

Sample internal communications audit

PREAMBLE

Depending on what online survey tool you use and how you propose to get it to your internal audience, there needs to be a preamble which introduces the Audit.

This may be in the email which conveys the link to the online tool (eg Survey Monkey) or could simply be a blurb on the Audit preceding the questions.

The preamble should:
- re-state the reason for the audit, ie to understand what works and what doesn't in internal comms and to seek improvements
- emphasise its confidential and anonymous nature
- give an idea of how long it will take to do (typically)
- identify when the audit is open to (date)

- explain what will be done with the findings and a timeframe for the process (ie once it's closed, how long to analyse, how long to prepare and agree any recommendations, and if possible when those will be announced and rolled out).

QUESTIONS

1. **Rate the IMPORTANCE to you of the information you receive in these areas:**
   - H&S information, including information on wellbeing
   - information about your own business or functional unit/department
   - information about how the company/organisation is doing and future plans
   - human interest information about people in the company/organisation
   - information about what the company/organisation is doing in the community and through its sponsorships, environmental or other corporate social responsibility (CSR) activities (if applicable)
   - social news relating to the company/organisation
   - information on new appointments, promotions, internal vacancies or new roles being established
   - information about the company/organisation globally (if part of a multi-national)

   Other areas may be added specific to your business/sector.

Very important / Quite important / Fairly important / Slightly important / Not important at all / Don't know

---

2. **Rate the QUALITY of the information you receive in these areas (use the same choices as Q1)**

Categories

Very good / Good / Fair / Poor / Very poor / Don't know

---

3. **Rate the AMOUNT of information you get in these areas (same choices as Q1)**

Categories

Too much / Plenty / Sufficient / Not enough / Hardly any / Don't know

---

4. **Rate the EFFECTIVENESS of the following internal communications tools, channels and activities in communicating information to you** (Note: these will vary depending on the organisation – below are general headings. You should be specific in referring to the tools/channels by their known name, eg newsletter title, intranet, company/organisation updates)
   • company/organisation newsletter (may be more than one entry for this if there are a number of newsletters)

- whole organisation meetings (ie company updates, town hall meetings)
- roadshows (if applicable)
- team meetings
- organisation/company intranet
- email announcements from senior management
- information from my manager/supervisor
- noticeboards
- social events
- social media (eg Facebook, Twitter, LinkedIn, Instagram, YouTube, Blogs)
- other tools, channels or activities (specify in the space below)

---

5. **What WORKS WELL in internal communications in this company/organisation?** (With space for respondent to write)

---

6. **If you were made responsible for internal communications in this company/organisation, what would be the first IMPROVEMENT you'd make?** (With space for respondent to write)

---

7. **How many opportunities are there for communications FROM EMPLOYEES TO MANAGEMENT** (ie bottom-up)?

Categories

Heaps! / Many / Some / Not many / Almost none / Don't know

---

8. What is your DEPARTMENT / UNIT / DIVISION ?*

List here would include the different functional parts of the organisation, eg corporate office (including Finance, IT), HR, H&S, Sales and Marketing, or could be business units within the company.

Depending on numbers within each area you may aggregate employees into larger groupings to preserve anonymity.

---

9. What is your ROLE?

List here could be in general terms, eg:
- non-managerial employee (no direct reports)
- senior manager (direct report to the executive team)
- middle Manager (manager of managers)
- line manager (manager of people, eg foreperson, supervisor)

Or specified roles could be more detailed to the function performed.

10. Where are you LOCATED?*

Include this question if you wish to identify different geographic viewpoints relating to the location of employees (Head Office, branches, external sites, workshops, etc).

*Again this question needs to take account of the need for replies to be anonymous.

---

11. Are there any other GENERAL COMMENTS about internal communications at this company / organisation you'd like to make? (With space for respondent to write answer)

CLOSE

Don't forget to end the Audit with a **thank you** to the respondents for taking the time to fill out the Survey, and reiterate the **Purpose**, **Value** and **Confidentiality** of the exercise.

Simple communications plan framework

SITUATION

- What's happened / is happening / will happen that calls for some serious comms planning? What's the problem?

OBJECTIVES

- What do you want to achieve from your communications? Where do you want the target audience(s) to get to in terms of awareness, understanding, acceptance, support, advocacy...?

KEY AUDIENCES AND MESSAGES

- Who are you trying to reach?

- What are the key things you want them to know, understand, agree with, argue for you…?

STRATEGIES

- How might you do this, if it's not an easy communication? How will you get cut-through?

TACTICS, TOOLS AND CHANNELS

- Breaking those Strategies down, what specific approaches will you take – using what tools and via what channels of communications?

ACTIONS

- To make that all happen, what are your action steps, with responsibilities and timings?
- What resources do you need? Can you get them?

EVALUATION

- How will you assess if you've successfully communicated what you needed to and if it's had the desired outcome?

Sample rap

Any basic rap beat will work as a backdrop to your lyrics; one I've used internally is St. Germain's *La Goutte D'Or* (off **Tourist**). But be aware that using any copyrighted music to, for example, put a rap video out on YouTube requires the musician's/composer's permission.

EXPECT A TRAIN

The railway line is a dangerous place
don't go there if you're off your face.
And if you need to cross the line
make sure that you obey the sign.

A train is big, a train is fast;
you feel the breeze when it goes past.
Don't walk the line – you're not Johnny Cash
cos get it wrong and….smash!

Chorus: Expect a train, expect a train;
respect the train and use your brain (repeat)

If the lights are on and the arms are down
gotta wait a while till the train is gone.
When the bells have stopped and the arms are high
you're good to drive to the other side.

Don't jump the gun with your headphones on;
no second chance if you get it wrong.
Take your time to check the track
stay vigilant - don't turn your back.

Chorus

Gotta be mad, to climb a train;
if you fall off, gonna cause you pain
and pain as well for the railway staff
who tidy up – and that's no laugh.

The shortest line might shorten your life.
Do you really want the trouble and strife?
Find your thrills in another place
and keep away from the railway space.

Chorus

Please treat the train like you ought to do
a comfy ride and a beautiful view,
a way to get from A to B
or to send your stuff down to the sea.

We're working hard to make Rail grow
but we need you to be in the know.
Be safe on the track and tell your friends
and don't forget how this rap ends.

"Don't walk the line, you're not Johnny Cash..." A still from the filming of "Expect a Train" (Photo courtesy The VC Company / Brendon O'Hagan)

BIBLIOGRAPHY

Larkin, TJ & Larkin, Sandar. (1994) *Communicating Change: Winning Employee Support for New Business Goals.* McGraw Hill.

Quirke, Bill. (2008) *Making the Connections: Using Internal Communication to Turn Strategy Into Action (Second Edition).* Routledge.

Quirke, Bill. (1996) *Communicating Corporate Change: A Practical Guide to Communication and Corporate Strategy.* McGraw-Hill.

Pink, Daniel H. (2009) *Drive: The Surprising Truth About What Motivates Us.* Riverhead.

Maurer, Rick. (2010) *Beyond the Wall of Resistance: Why 70% of All Changes Still Fail - and What You Can Do About It.* Bard Press.

Pennington, Randy. (2013) *Making Change Work: Staying Nimble, Relevant, and Engaged in a World of Constant Change.* Wiley.

Barrett, Richard. (2014) *The Values-Driven Organization: Unleashing Human Potential for Performance and Profit.* Routledge.

The Economist. (2005) *The Economist Style Guide.* Bloomberg

My apologies that this bibliography is thin. Truth is, there wasn't much in book form that I could see out there focusing on this topic in any helpful depth.

Not specific to a New Zealand context anyway. What you read in this book is largely drawn from my own and others' experience of what happens in internal comms, and what does (and doesn't) work.

There are a number of professional comms practitioners who do great work in this area, however, and I would like to acknowledge the untiring efforts of the Public Relations Institute of New Zealand (PRINZ) in supporting the industry with workshops and conference papers on the subject and practice, in particular Elizabeth Hughes who ran a very practical and informative internal comms workshop I attended some years ago and who continues to fly the flag high for internal comms, along with the tireless Catherine Arrow.

REFERENCES

1   Larkin & Larkin, *Communicating Change*, p 148.

2   George Orwell, "Politics and the English Language",
    Horizon (Vol. 13, Issue 76, April 1946), pp 252–
    265.

3   Wan How, *Master 4D Time Management* (Amazon
    2015).

4   Keith Ferrazi, "Candour, Criticism, Teamwork",
    Harvard Business Review (Jan-Feb 2012) p 40.

5   Pink, *Drive*, p 48.

6   Maurer, *Beyond the Wall of Resistance*, pp 30-32.

7   Quirke, *Communicating Corporate Change*, p 115.

8   Larkin and Larkin, *Communicating Change*,
    Introduction, xi.

INDEX

17417865R00079

Printed in Great Britain
by Amazon